# THE BIBLE AND MONEY

*Allen Hollis*

HAWTHORN BOOKS, INC.
**Publishers** / NEW YORK

Scripture quotations are from the Revised Standard Version of the Bible, copyrighted 1946, 1952, © 1971, 1973 by the Division of Education and Ministry of the National Council of the Churches of Christ in the United States of America.

THE BIBLE AND MONEY

Copyright © 1976 by Allen Hollis. Copyright under International and Pan-American Copyright Conventions. All rights reserved, including the right to reproduce this book or portions thereof in any form, except for the inclusion of brief quotations in a review. All inquiries should be addressed to Hawthorn Books, Inc., 260 Madison Avenue, New York, New York 10016. This book was manufactured in the United States of America and published simultaneously in Canada by Prentice-Hall of Canada, Limited, 1870 Birchmount Road, Scarborough, Ontario.

Library of Congress Catalog Card Number: 75-41798

ISBN: 0-8015-0616-6

1 2 3 4 5 6 7 8 9 10

Dedicated to my father and grandfather
for giving me some of the background
that enabled me to write this book

# Contents

**1**
The Bible and Money — 3

**2**
Teachings in Leviticus, Deuteronomy, Kings — 12

**3**
Teachings in Proverbs and Psalms — 24

**4**
Money and the Prophets — 39

**5**
Jesus' Teaching about Money — 54

**6**
The Rest of the New Testament — 72

**7**
Major Biblical Themes                                94

**8**
A Theology of Money                                 111

# THE BIBLE AND MONEY

# 1
# *The Bible and Money*

Money is a religious problem. In fact, it has been a problem ever since Old Testament times. There have been periods in which money was looked on as more evil than sex. There were periods when money was considered to be the just and proper fruit of virtue, as exemplified in some of the Calvinist churches.

As religious people have wrestled with this problem over the years, the old adage that the devil can cite Scripture for his own purpose seems particularly true. Even if we leave the devil out of the argument, certainly human beings have not been backward in extolling scriptural passages that bolster their instincts and prejudices and ignoring those that point in other directions. Interpreting theology, for some, is like doing jigsaw puzzles, with the freedom to reshape the pieces when they do not fit easily.

Happily, many theologians have avoided this trap, but the average layman in the church, as well as many outside the church, would be horrified at the way arguments have been constructed to justify all manner of strange conclusions. Most people simply do not read enough, and the professional religious people who do soon learn not to inquire too far lest they become confused or, worse yet, offer too many alternatives to their flocks. Truth, for most, is far more palatable if offered as three simple points, even if distortion results.

But, even though the risks are great, it is important to try to work out the framework of the Christian faith intelligently. While it is not necessary to be a mental giant to be a Christian, we must, at least, start with a minimal rational framework, or else we are at the mercy of the devil in our feelings. Not that I am against feelings—faith without emotion is sterile and, worse yet, deadly dull. But this rational framework is needed, largely for those whose primary reception of reality is through their intellect, to a much lesser degree for those who absorb more knowledge through their senses or through intuition.

In the case of money there has been relatively less biblical study done than in many other areas of life. Volumes have been written about sex and the faith, about war, and about a generous number of other topics, but very little about money.

It is surprising that there has been so little systematic thinking about what Christians should do about money. Money affects us all. If we have too little, we feel deprived and, in extreme cases, may suffer great hardships. Even when we have enough for a comfortable standard of living, it is a rare person who does not feel that a higher income would be preferable. When a person is rich by the standards of a given society, there is the further problem of how to conserve money and at the same time make it work most effectively.

At first glance, it seems strange that relatively little has been written about money from a Christian perspective. The first reason for this is that most Christians feel a peculiar ambivalence about money. They like it, and yet it causes problems. As we shall discover, there is more written on this in a negative vein in the Bible than in a positive one. From a Biblical perspective, there are all kinds of reasons why it is wrong to seek and conserve money. Yet, material creatures that we are, we know that to eat, to be sheltered, and to wear clothes requires it. Preachers on the one hand thunder about its evils; on the other hand, they ask for generous contributions to their institutions. Such an approach suggests that when the church has money, it is less evil somehow, less tainted than when an individual possesses it. If the church were run by angels, there might be no problems. But it is run by people, and money is a problem in all churches. There is an ambivalence about the subject that leaves people clinging to platitudes and getting along as best they can. I think we can do better.

The second reason is that the Bible has relatively little to say about money. I have made a fairly exhaustive analysis of the subject, and most of the pertinent passages will come under our scrutiny in the following chapters. But there just are not very many passages on the subject, and no even modestly lengthy discourses on the issue, so it is hard to write volumes. Biblical interpreters have shown enormous ingenuity in building elaborate superstructures on minimal foundations. More often than not these elaborate structures come crashing down after a time.

I think it better to be prudent about Biblical conclusions, as indeed for all conclusions, and I hope that people will avoid the nearly irresistible urge to stretch for conclusions unsupported by evidence, and I have tried not to write too little or too much.

The ambivalence people feel about money is also reflected in the Bible, and that is the third reason for the lack of writing on this subject. Most Christian theologians—and even more Christian lay people—abhore ambivalence. Loose ends in faith scare people to death, and when the Bible gives testimony in more than one direction on a subject, people become confused. The prohibition of killing in the Ten Commandments is countered by numerous succeeding passages in Exodus that prescribe various reasons for invoking the death penalty. Preachers have been trying to get around that problem for centuries. Passages about money are even more ambiguous, and reconciling them is extremely difficult.

The fourth reason is more speculative, but it strikes me as pertinent. The Bible was written in a period of time and in an area of the world that was not wealthy. For a brief time, in the reign of King Solomon, the kingdom generated some wealth, and during this period of the prophets there was a small upper class that had some luxuries. But our version of middle-class comfort did not exist—and those not in the top class were quite poor.

How poor is a matter of conjecture. There is virtually no reference to the wholesale grinding poverty we associate with such Asian cities as Calcutta, where people literally starve in the streets. There is no reference to starvation in the concordances. By inference, and with some reservations, it seems reasonable to believe that abject poverty was not an overwhelming problem. Jesus did say that the poor would be always with us, but I find no signs that poverty was a major problem, save, perhaps, in times of great famine. The majority subsisted at a minimal level, but they endured.

When the large majority of people had only enough money or goods to live at a minimal level, there was very little reason to spend much time thinking about money. Furthermore, there was no real expectation that enough could be generated so that the majority would live comfortably. They could not conceive of a system which could generate capital through the increased productivity of machinery. What they had was done by human hands. There was no thought, no dream of economic progress. So the problems connected with money were of an extremely limited nature as compared with the many other problems of living. Bible writers, therefore, dealt with the problems of the times: interest, fairness, and barter.

For these four reasons relatively little has been written about the Bible and money. That which has appeared has often been written to support preconceived conclusions, such as when the Puritans argued about the virtues of money-making.

But today the need to do so is great, because we live in a very different kind of world economically. I think we need to take a look at what this world is like. Let us start with the poor, who are still with us. There are all kinds of government guidelines, which tell us what poverty is, but they do not tell the real story. When I walk through Boston Common, I often see people, mostly men, lying on cement benches. They wear ragged clothes, they are filthy, they look unhappy, and they are poor. For some, those benches are their beds. These are only a handful, but there are thousands living on welfare. They live in shoddy apartments, with running water and toilets that don't work very well. Many have inadequate diets, though how much is due to lack of money and how much to lack of knowledge varies. Much to the chagrin of the righteous, most of them have TV sets. They are poor and they feel poor. However, their lives are far more comfortable than those of the thousands I have seen sleeping on the sidewalks in Bombay. I remember a cartoon in an Indian magazine, which showed a post office worker receiving an award for delivering the mail accurately to people who lived on the sidewalks.

Our conception of poverty is, therefore, very different from the poverty of the Old and New Testament, or the rest of today's world. Our poverty is relative luxury, which doesn't mean that the poor should feel lucky. It is psychologically more painful to be poor in an affluent country than it is to be poor in a poor country, where the majority are in the same boat and expectations are not as high.

If our poverty is different, our affluence is unbelievably different. Our world is full of money. Even in these inflationary times we need to appreciate the incredible amount of money that is available to many people. We take it for granted, but the way we live is a phenomenon in the history of the human race, even though it is limited to a minority of the world's inhabitants.

Not only is there a lot of money, there is what is known as credit. Consider how many of our daily transactions are based on the amazing premise that someone has promised to pay at some future date. You often hear it said that you can't trust anyone any more, but that is simply not true. Our whole economic system is built on trust. Most of our transactions consist of pieces of paper with signatures, which have no inherent value. Their only value lies in the fact that we trust people will render something of value in exchange for goods and services. I would be the first to admit that some people take advantage of this system, but I think they are remarkably few. The credit system, which is the promise to pay, and so far exceeds anything ever seen on earth, is a major area of economic reality that was unknown to the Bible writers.

Another remarkable phenomenon is the inherent worthlessness of money today. When the ancient Hebrews paid in terms of grain and oil, those items had an inherent worth, for they could be eaten. As the art of commerce developed, gold and silver became the mediums of exchange and, because of their rarity and durability, they were considered valuable. Jewels, too, have been valued by most cultures because of their beauty and durability.

There is a problem in giving a precise definition of today's money. It is a medium of exchange through which a person can buy or sell services and goods. Are checking accounts money? Are credit cards money? There are divided opinions on these subjects, and the arguments that abound are almost as abstruse as the ones given by medieval theologians. These pieces of paper have no inherent value. They have value because people feel they are valuable. Inflation occurs when people become unsure of where value really lies. The value of money goes down and down, following Gresham's old law that bad money drives out good. We are not subject to many of the problems that were present in pre-Civil War days, when every bank and every state could print its own money, but we are plagued still with the problem of trusting a medium whose value is essentially based on faith.

Another factor that makes today's life very different is our vastly increased productivity. The ancient Hebrews were limited to what they could design with their hands and what they could cultivate in the fields, and the Bible writers did not have to contend with the depersonalizing effects on people of this massive juggernaut of productivity. We are used to the marvels of machines and chemistry; but in the underdeveloped areas of the world, which do not have electricity, motorized transport, chemical fertilizers, and all those things we take for granted, productivity is limited. One reason that we are rapidly slowing down in being able to create new wealth is that we seem to have reached a limit in what our machines can do for us. There may be other kinds of breakthroughs, but their ultimate effectiveness will hinge on our ability to supply energy to them, and that prospect is not as bright as it was.

Our previous thought leads to another phenomenon unknown to Bible writers, the enormous concentration of economic power in giant industrial firms. Making accurate comparisons is impossible, but it does not seem unreasonable to imagine that even a smaller firm like American Motors has more total worth than all of biblical Israel. We do not have any detailed picture of how Solomon operated what was a sophisticated business operation during his reign, though we are sure it quite surpassed anything previously seen. But it was small potatoes to our firms. And most business was fragmented, farmers, shop keepers, miners, tree cutters, nothing in comparison to ITT.

As we face the problems of understanding how the Bible can speak to a world so different, we must be aware of the differences. How would Jesus have framed parables in the commercial world of today? How could he envisage a world of computers that provide immediate answers? He couldn't. He lived in a world of farms and shops, in a dry and unproductive land. Yet the human insights contained in the Bible are just as valid today as they ever were. Our problem is to find out what these insights are, and then to see how they apply.

So let us set off on a journey through the Scriptures to see what is said about money and what conclusions we can draw from this. The mercifully anonymous wit who said that theology is like finding a bat in a dark room was painfully close to the truth in some respects, but if we can look on our task as shedding light in a dark room, then we will not wander too far afield. Money is too important to all for us not to have a solid biblical understanding of the subject, even if we do not all come to the same conclusion from the evidence available.

### For Further Thought

Those who like to deal with questions while they read might well pause for a moment and ask where they are with respect to their understanding of money. Do you ever make any serious attempts to link your Christian faith with how you handle your money or how you feel about your money? Is a poor person an inherently lower moral type in your mind? What are the foundations of your understanding of money? We all make an incredible number of assumptions about money, as indeed we do about everything, and we increase in our knowledge and understanding only when we become fully aware of these assumptions, which have been part of our lives for years. Sometimes, just by asking ourselves what we assume about something, we discover that we have been operating under conceptions that do not correspond to reality. Take a good look at all your basic assumptions about money, write them down if necessary, and then proceed to the biblical data that follows.

# 2
# *Teachings in Leviticus, Deuteronomy, Kings*

It may not be chronologically correct to begin an analysis of the Old Testament passages about money at the beginning of the Bible, but it does offer us a familiar pattern, which we can accept easily. The reason it may not be chronologically correct is because the first passages, which pertain to money, show up in Leviticus, a book of common law finally drawn together after the Exile, which contains laws and practices going back, in some cases, to the times of Moses himself.

It seems reasonable to assume that the passages that concern us in Lev. 25 come from a period when Israel was established in the cities and that they are not as old as Moses. The clue for this thought comes from Lev. 25:29, which refers to the sale of a dwelling house in a walled city. Obviously there would be no need for a law about the transaction of property in cities until the Hebrews were well established in such places. The exact date is unimportant as long as we can appreciate that we are not dealing with Israel in its nomadic state and that some significant degree of urbanization has taken place.

## Teachings in Leviticus, Deuteronomy, Kings

The first passage in this book for us is Lev. 25:35-37:

> And if your brother becomes poor and cannot maintain himself with you, you shall maintain him; as a stranger and sojourner he shall live with you. Take no interest from him or increase, but fear your God; that your brother may live beside you. You shall not lend him your money at interest, nor give him your food for profit.

The problem of interest rates is not a new one. We know that most of the ancient cultures with a money system had incorporated the lending of money at interest into the economic system. These rates were steep, depending on the security and nature of the loan, but 20 to 40 percent could be considered a normal range. Human nature being what it has always been, there always have been those who tried to get even more for their money, and rules have arisen to deal with human greed in this context.

We see in the above passage one of these rules as it applies to families. The first rule about money is that you must not charge your brother interest. The fact that such a rule existed at all is a strong indication that some sharp operators had charged interest to family members, and somehow, to the Hebrew lawmakers, such a practice was not in the best interests of family solidarity. There is certainly a sense in which charging interest when a brother has become poor is taking advantage in the worst possible way. The law is a good indication of the way the Hebrews felt about the importance of the family and the need to keep it together, even when one of the members has suffered a reversal. There is no prohibition against loaning money within the family; such an act might be a very helpful one, which would ultimately strengthen the family position.

It is always a temptation in theology to deduce, infer, or extract too much from a given passage, but at the same time the attempt must be made in order to increase knowledge. The point I want to highlight here is that people are always tempted to increase the amount of money they have. Interest is the way money makes more money; and since it is not the money itself that has desires, but the people who have it, the early laws with regard to money first had to deal with the temptation to make money out of money and in the passage we are considering, to make money out of the misfortune of a brother. This early law was designed to control greed.

It is well to keep in mind also what the passage does not say. It is not a blanket prohibition against charging any kind of interest. We know that the commercial interests of Israel charged interest to business customers, and there is no question but what this practice was perfectly acceptable. No doubt there were codes governing what could be charged, and no doubt there were those on the fringes who were ready to charge more than the usual rate in tense circumstances. Such people are always around the fringes of commerce. The issue is not the goodness of money in and of itself, the issue is the control of human drives to maximize a money situation.

Another interesting passage is from Lev. 27:16-25, which is a lengthy description of the various ways a person could dedicate property to the Lord, and the means by which such gifts were evaluated, and possibly even regained by the donor. It was possible to donate a field to the Lord and later to purchase it back by giving a fifth more above the purchase price to the priests. Of course there are many many laws in Exodus and Leviticus about the various ways that people could and should contribute to the religious enterprise, but more often in the Hebrew culture such gifts were in terms of produce and not money. It may be that this passage is rather later than some of the others.

Whatever the date, it is important to note that the religious establishment was concerned about its own support, first in terms of animals and grain and later, as in this section, in terms of money. This theme is present in every major organized religion we know. There is always provision within the religious system for the support of the religious establishment, whether it is a Hindu temple or a Christian church. The rationale for the support can be expressed in a variety of ways, but the end product is always the same—the believer has a duty to give part of his wealth to the religious institution. Those who do not contribute are made to feel guilty or deficient, and in some situations they are dismissed from membership.

It is too early in our exploration to draw hard and fast conclusions about money from this one illustration, but a few observations may help. This area of religion is prone to bring out the cynicism in people very fast. Sooner or later, in every church, some individual or group becomes upset over the fact that the authorities are always pressing them about money. If it is not the local parish it is the denomination, and it usually seems to be both. Except in the case of great endowments, it seldom seems that there is enough money to run the machinery. Leaving aside how other religions handle these feelings, we must simply acknowledge that there is always tension in the life of the church with regard to money. Whatever else the church may teach about money, it is concerned with having enough of it to operate in the manner it would like.

I do not think the situation has been helped by the ambiguous teachings of the church in this regard, and I know as a local pastor that there are plenty of times when I become cynical about the constant effort needed to raise money for operating funds, as well as for the special drives, always for good causes. But I would like to keep my cynicism in check for the moment, because obviously this ancient phenomena extends beyond Christendom, though it may not be as stringent in other religions. As we see it extending far back into Hebrew history, we will be far better off if we admit that it is a point of enduring tension and look for a theological approach that will minimize some of the conflicts we now endure.

Later in the religious practice of Israel came the concept of the tithe, first found in Deuteronomy. References to tithing in Leviticus and in Numbers are thought to be fairly late additions. We can take Deuteronomy 14:22ff as illustrative:

> You shall tithe all the yield of your seed . . . and if the way is too long for you so that you are not able to bring the tithe . . . then you shall turn it into money, and bind up the money in your hand and go to the place where he will chose . . .

God was considered to be the owner of the land and therefore entitled to a tenth of its yield. It is a very specific application of our previous consideration of the support of the religious establishment. The concept of a tenth seems to be arbitrary from a religious point of view, but it probably was a reasonable kind of assessment on the landowners, achievable by a sufficient number of people to make the system work, large enough to give a sense of significance and value to the religious establishment, yet not so large as to make people rebellious. Unless people have changed a lot since those days, there were probably some who gave much less, some who gave the right amount, and a few generous souls who gave more.

There was no magic in the giving of the grains and animals, because the law describes the opportunity by which a person who would have a difficult time getting all that produce to the central sanctuary could change the goods into money, which could be carried easily by hand. Not so much in Israel as in many other primitive cultures, people originally thought that the products of the land would be pleasing to God in and of themselves. As time went on, the giving centered on the feelings accompanying the giving and on the support of the religious establishment. We can reasonably assume in the wording of this law that both the sense of God's ownership of the land and the need for giving were being honored. The fruits of the land were preferred; but if they could not be delivered directly, then the money was adequate.

This passage allows us to build upon our previous theme of supporting the institution. Our religious heritage early identified the need to encourage people to give. Money is something many people instinctively want to possess. Religion quickly identified the fact that if there is no pressure put on people to be generous and outgoing with their money, all too many will tend to become ingrown and stingy, and this tendency is not a productive one in human beings. Therefore, even in the most primitive religions, there is almost always a provision for the giving of something to the deity. In the beginning of many religions, this need for giving was all mixed up with some other themes. It is hard to interpret human sacrifice as being expanding to the human spirit, and how it could ever be thought of as pleasing to the deity is something quite beyond the conception of most of us in the twentieth century.

But when we cut away some of the excesses, we find that theme of giving of things of value over and over again. To put it in modern psychological terms, which would not have been thought of in the ancient past, the giving of money is therapeutic because when people give up something that is valuable, which does not offer them some very immediate return of value, such as the purchase of food or a television set, they are pulled out beyond themselves, forced to think in terms beyond immediate self-gratification and directed toward something exceedingly remote, like God. Most people are not very conscious of this fact, many fight being urged to give, but when you stop to consider how many people respond to the religious call to give, even reluctantly, it becomes hard to ignore the role that giving plays in the life of people. An adequate theology of money must take into account this theme, which seems so deeply ingrained in the religious activity of people across the ages.

Another theme from the early books is the theme of fairness with money, which we may find in Deut. 25:13-15:

> You shall not have in your bag two kinds of weights, a large and a small. You shall not have in your house two kinds of measures, a large and a small. A full and just weight you shall have, a full and just measure you shall have; that your days may be prolonged in the land which the Lord Your God gives you.

It is hard at this distance in time to know accurately how honest or corrupt business practices were in urban Israel at any given point. The Old Testament gives clues to corruption at various times, as we will see when we consider what the prophets had to say on the subject of wealth, but how extensive sharp practices might have been is hard to judge. Nevertheless, this law was not written in a vacuum, and we may legitimately infer that there was a need for it, to control the urge to cheat.

The religious and legal authorities understood the need for fairness and trust within the community. When people cannot trust one another, be it in business or politics, the fabric of society begins to unravel very fast, a point much at issue in this country at this moment. The temptation to maximize the amount of money within a transaction is strong. We saw it in the matter of interest rates, now we see it with respect to weights and measures. Weights and measures would have had even more economic significance in daily transactions in Hebrew society than in ours, since grains, oils, and other produce all had to be hand measured in the marketplace. Not that we are without such problems, as evidenced by such items as air-filled cereal boxes. There is apparently a never-ending fight to insure fair measure.

Therefore, there were very early laws designed to ensure fairness in economic dealings, and such laws had a religious as well as a secular sanction. Those familiar with the Old Testament concept of law will take such a comment for granted, but for those not so familiar with the laws of the Old Testament, the religious foundation of Hebrew law, it simply needs to be pointed out. There was not the division between religious and secular law that we now have.

It may seem odd to many in the twentieth century that God could be concerned about anything as trivial as weights and measures, and there are always those who doubt that God has any concern for the commercial, choosing to ignore the prophets on this point. But if God is a deity of morality and justice, then he is concerned about all activities of men that involve morality and justice. Simply because an item is small in the cosmic scheme of things does not mean that it is overlooked by a God who is consistently and passionately concerned for human behavior. It is true that many of the laws found in the Old Testament have very limited application, such as laws concerning leprosy. But laws that involve trust and honesty reach far beyond the Hebrew culture and may truly be said to be rooted in the divine, which we perceive, uncertainly in some situations, as being concerned with the morality of man. Therefore, this law about giving fair weight, so as not to cheat people out of their money, gives us good reason to believe that God is concerned with fairness in economic dealings, so people may trust each other. We perhaps can hold at this point to a tentative thought that God is concerned for honesty with respect to money and watch as we go along to see if the theme repeats itself.

The last passage to consider in this chapter is I Kings 10:14–29. Though it is not taken from the Pentateuch, it belongs to the earlier days of the Hebrews. Some of the laws we have discussed may have been from the same period, so it is not out of place to include it here. The passage is a description of the wealth that Solomon brought his kingdom. If it is true that the gold brought to Solomon in one year was 666 talents, we are dealing with about $16 million in gold, if gold is worth $35 an ounce. Given the present confusion in the world's gold market, it is hard to be more precise, except to note that, at free-market prices, it would be worth much much more. In any event, the exact dollar figure is relatively unimportant. What is important is that we are looking at a very affluent situation, where millions and millions of dollars are flowing through the kingdom.

Solomon was not prone to conceal the wealth that the kingdom enjoyed. He made shields of gold, obviously for show, because a gold shield would be too heavy and soft for a fight. He had an ivory throne with gold overlay. Gold vessels adorned the royal table, and perhaps the crowning touch is given in I Kings 14–21: "... nowhere of silver, it was not considered as anything in the days of Solomon." When silver is not worth anything, affluence truly abounds! To what degree, if any, the author is guilty of exaggerating the wealth of the kingdom it is impossible to determine, but there seems no good reason to doubt that under Solomon's admitted genius for organization and commerce the lavishness of the stories are within the bounds of reason.

The decline of the kingdom was not because Solomon had

built up great riches. The kingdom declined because Solomon took up with foreign women. Those who look for a sign of the corruption of wealth will not find it here. The Deuteronomy-oriented author of Kings had no visible problems with the wealth. It was God-given, because Solomon had been obedient to God and fully used the outstanding wisdom that God had given him. What was serious was the falling away from Yahweh and the introduction of women who worshipped other gods, a double theme of both the woman as corrupter and the terrible danger of a foreign deity.

From a more dispassionate vantage point in the present, it is quite possible to point out that such vast wealth must have had a corrupting influence on Solomon, making him less zealous about his faith than he might have been. I would offer a subjective personal opinion, based on an admittedly limited knowledge of human nature, that such corruption by wealth is all too possible, and I cannot imagine that it would not have affected Solomon. But that is the reaction of a twentieth-century Protestant and is not in harmony with the author.

What is truly significant in the quest for the Christian understanding of money is that here is a place where, if ever there was a glowing chance to identify the evils surrounding money, this story is it. But instead, the whole story of Solomon is a story about how wealth may flow to those who are obedient to God. It is a pre-Puritan capitalist story, which would be the delight of the industrial giants of today, if any of them read enough of the Bible to understand it. Our acceptance of this passage as part of the appropriate biblical material is important in building a full Christian understanding of money and, as we will see later, it would have made analysis simpler if we had ignored it. It is difficult to be honest in the work of theology. We must accept the fact that

*The Bible and Money*

wealth for this biblical author was a virtue, a result of God-pleasing efforts to which Solomon and his kingdom were entitled, which they could display lavishly, even vulgarly by many standards.

### For Further Thought

An interesting question to ponder is what degree of control needs to be placed on money. For instance, banks are currently restricted by law from giving more than a certain amount on interest rates. Why shouldn't a bank be allowed to offer whatever interest rates it thinks best? There may be a few souls who think that there need not be any controls at all, but I think most people feel the need for some. But how many and how strong do they need to be?

Those questions lead to another one. If everyone had an adequate income, would we need as many controls? I grant that the use of the word adequate is subject to varying degrees of understanding, but the fact that in our society there are people who do not have an adequate income by any reasonable standard means that there are subtle pressures on the cost of money. It is human nature to try to take advantage of the disadvantage of people in need, the strongest example being the one of loan sharks, who will lend money to desperate people who cannot obtain it in any other way. If we all had enough, would the need for controls increase or diminish?

A final question can be addressed primarily to those who are part of the church, though it is often one reason why some avoid the church. Does the insistence of the religious institution on support from its members represent a great fraud, or a great opportunity? There would be some who would argue that there is not a need for a religious institution. But the bulk of human experience argues otherwise, and so far no sizable religious group has avoided the institution. How much support should it have, and why? You may have changed your mind by the time you finish the book, but tackle it early in the light of these ancient passages showing the need for financial support of the religious establishment.

# 3
# *Teachings in Proverbs and Psalms*

Psalms and Proverbs offer some interesting material on the subject of money, though it is clear that money, wealth, and riches were not of primary interest to the authors. The references in the Psalms are significant in that they represent how prayerful Hebrew people felt about the world in which they lived, as men poured out their hearts about the things of life that concerned them most. Proverbs provides material that is much less from the heart and more from the head, and in modern terms might be considered the conventional moral wisdom of Israel.

Unfortunately it is not easy to pin down dates for this material, which in turn makes it hard to fit individual references to particular times in the history of Israel. The Psalms were composed over a very long period. Some of them may go all the way back to David, though most scholars are reasonably well satisfied that he did not write as many as are directly attributed to him. The final compilation took place between 400 and 200 B.C. Proverbs is likewise a composition covering many many years. Here we are more confident of attributing much of the material to Solomon, but many additions were made in later years, and the bulk of Proverbs was composed between the 900s B.C., when Solomon reigned, and the Exile in the sixth century, B.C.

I think we can be comfortable if we can identify these books as being the products of the urban kingdom of Israel between the great kings and the Exile, a settled, organized period of history unpleasantly punctuated by frequent wars. In that period there was a well-organized economy involving commerce and mining. The kingdom had known a rich period under Solomon, but it seems to have fallen back economically after his death.

The first reference to our subject is found in Ps. 15:5. The question at the head of this psalm is who shall live in the Lord's tent and dwell in his holy hill. In less anthropomorphic terms, the question is who shall be close to God. One of the qualifications according to v. 5 is that such a person will not put his money out at interest. There is not much to go on here, and it would be unwise to draw too many conclusions. The sentence does not indicate whether this thought is a repeat of the passage against charging interest to one's own brother, or whether it is a blanket prohibition against interest in general. From what we know generally about the way business was conducted, those outside of Israel had better have been on their guard when it came to interest rates. It seems more likely that the passage reflects the laws against usurious interest rates for fellow countrymen and particularly for family members.

Thus we have another example of the emphasis laid on fair business practices within the community. Money must be handled with restraint. To those of us in modern times, it may look rather strange to limit such restraint to the country. However, I would note just in passing, we have only recently

*The Bible and Money*

entered into a world where the interlocking economic community needs as strong restraints on a worldwide scale as Israel did within her boundaries.

A new theme is introduced in Ps. 49:5–12. The author writes movingly about the inevitability of death, observing, almost casually, that the rich cannot take it with them, summed up with the poignant words in v. 12: "Man cannot abide in his pomp, he is like the beasts which perish." At a feeling level, there are so many people who would like to take their money with them when they pass from this earth. Rationally they know they cannot, that the time will come when they must leave what they have to others. But many people fight that fact. The ancient Egyptian pyramids reflected this human desire when the Pharaohs were buried with great wealth around them, presumably so that they would have it to use in the next life. This theme can be traced right down to a wonderful cartoon, which appeared in *The New Yorker* some years ago, showing a funeral procession in which the funeral and flower cars were followed by several armoured cars. Two men are standing on the sidewalk watching this bizarre procession, and one says to the other, "I see old Smedly is trying to take it with him!"

I will leave the detailed analysis of why we try to hold onto our money even into death to the psychologists. But it is certainly true that the major religions of the world have taught that you can't take it with you, and that people should see wealth in very transitory terms. It does not last forever, it can be lost so very easily. To cling to it beyond the realm of reason is to turn it into a god, which can be very demonic and unhealthy. This passage is by no means the only time this theme shows up, and we will return to it again.

The fragility of wealth is set forth in a different key in Ps. 52:1–7. The psalmist is talking to a mighty man and predicting that God will bring him down. He closes his fiery speech with these sharp words:

> The righteous shall see and fear, and shall laugh at him, saying, See the man who would not make God his refuge, but trusted in the abundance of his riches and sought refuge in his wealth.

Here the psalmist addresses another problem people have with money. People try to use money as a shield. To some extent money is a shield, and it would be much too idealistic to say otherwise. Money can and does afford several kinds of protection. It offers protection against many kinds of physical discomfort. In our society it affords a measure of protection against disease. The simple ability to afford a regular medical examination may mean the difference between being able to diagnose disease in its early stages, when it is relatively easy to handle, and having to deal with it when it becomes extremely serious.

But people very quickly go beyond these forms of protection and use money as a form of psychological protection. They try to buy happiness and become frustrated when it does not work. They try to buy security against all kinds of pain, and it does not work. The psalmist saw that this mighty man was one of these people and knew that there was no secure refuge for this man in his wealth. Wealth is a shield, but a limited one.

Of all the books in the Bible, Proverbs provides the most positive view of money. Money is not the dominant theme of the book by any means. Wisdom or understanding is the principal theme, which should not be a surprise in light of the fact that much of the material was either composed or inspired by Solomon. While it is now impossible to know exactly which passages might be properly attributed to the wealthy king, it is easy, in a noncritical sense, to see how the book could have been written by Solomon, given his avowed sense of judgment. As we shall see, the blessings of wealth are not unqualified, but even the qualifications seldom renounce the positive values the book gives to the accumulation of wealth.

We can start with an excellent example of such qualification with Prov. 13:11: "Wealth hastily gotten will dwindle, but he who gathers little by little will increase it." That is a piece of folk wisdom that finds many counterparts right down to the Wall Street saying that pigs wind up with nothing. It is a very practical piece of wisdom, which very well could have come from Solomon himself. I suspect that the passage has more to do with the problems of human discipline than anything else. So very many people are out to accumulate money as fast as they can, as evidenced by the large number of people who play the lotteries, the punchboards, or the horses. They are looking for quick wealth. If they get it, they seem to have the knack of going through it, often in the pursuit of even quicker wealth. Gambling casinos know this human frailty, which is why they are not too nervous when someone makes a big killing. Granted they have the protection of the mathematical odds over the long pull, they also know that ninety-nine out of a hundred big winners will be back the next night to lose it all.

I can contrast this approach with that of a good gambler I knew when I was in seminary. He was an ardent poker player, and a consistent long-term winner. One of the qualities that made him successful was his patience and his willingness to accumulate his winnings over a long period. To be sure, he had the attributes of a successful gambler. He stayed away from games of pure chance and gambled only where skill played a significant role. He was a brilliant man, with great powers of concentration and observation. But he was patient, never fighting the cards, never trying to win when it was clear he was beaten.

So even the good gamblers know the wisdom of this verse. It is not necessary to give divine credit for it, because any good psychologist knows its truth. Yet it somehow has some significance for our investigation because it speaks of the need for control in our dealings with money. Control comes partially from knowledge, and so teachings like this one fill an important function in our learning how to deal with money, or with anything else for that matter.

Prov. 13 gets more positive toward wealth as it goes along. When we come to v. 18, we read: "Poverty and disgrace comes to him who ignores instruction, but he who heeds reproof is honored." Much of Proverbs is given to extolling the virtue of wisdom and judgment and the need for sound teaching of the young. There are rewards and punishments for learning the lessons, and here poverty is the reward for failure to heed wise instruction. It does not specifically say that wealth is the fruit of heeding wise instruction, but it is certainly implied. Rewards are very concrete in Proverbs. Doubtless there could be an argument over the precise meaning of the word *honored* in this context. It could be interpreted as the direct opposite of disgrace and imply that people will look up to those who heed instruction. But as the word lies also in the same relation to poverty, it seems reasonable to assume that honored carries with it the opposite of poverty as well. I do not want to press the issue too far.

But the verse is not far from a much clearer verse, v. 21, which says: "Misfortune pursues sinners, but prosperity rewards the righteous." It is hard to be more specific than that. Misfortune is the fruit of sin, and prosperity is the fruit of righteousness. It is possible to spiritualize the saying all out of context and say that prosperity should be interpreted in terms of a rich spiritual life; but if Solomon wrote this verse, or if it were inspired by his career, that interpretation can hardly stand up. Prosperity means just what Solomon would want it to mean, wealth; and we must handle the passage in that context. Certainly the Puritans did, as they accumulated their wealth in the rum trade.

Wealth as the product of virtue is a very attractive proposition. It legitimizes wealth and turns it into a positive good. The wealthy man no longer has to justify what he has because he can simply accept the fact that he would not have it unless he had been good. In crass terms he can have his cake and eat it too—his goodness and his wealth—with one confirming the other. It also gives the wealthy a reason for being less than compassionate about the poor, for if indeed a person is poor, it is a sign that he must have sinned somewhere along the way. Therefore, sympathy need not be wasted. It is small wonder that this passage is a favorite of the wealthy, though in this day and age, it occurs to very few to try and legitimize their wealth by appeal to the Scriptures. Still, there is something soothing about being able to be harmonious with Scripture, even when most people ignore it.

I think we need to ask a question to put the passage in its proper perspective, that question being: How true is the verse? How much human misfortune is attributable to sin, and how much human wealth is attributable to being good? The answer is partially subjective and very complex. But let me throw out some observations on the subject, and you can argue with me at your leisure. The three friends of Job express a theme found in many parts of the Old Testament, which describes suffering and misfortune as the consequence of sin. That view seems to be the conventional wisdom of Israel, and while it is not quite so conventional in our society, there are plenty of such feelings around. Probably they are not as strong in our culture because of the work of such great psychotherapists as Freud and Jung, who showed the great power of the unconscious with respect to people's activities.

There is an element of truth to this view, which I suspect that a few extremists would like to repudiate. These extremists are very leery of man's responsibility, feeling, in a way that distorts Freud, that the unconscious removes the bulk of human responsibility. However, those people who must deal with many of the unfortunate in our society can describe at length the cases in which people wind up in trouble because of their own weaknesses. They may be lazy and just not want to work. They may have a weakness for alcohol or other drugs, which prohibits them from participating in the normal workings of our society at best and at worst makes them enemies of society as they injure others to fulfill their needs. Even accepting all the ills of society, even being willing to stand in the prophetic tradition with respect to them, anarchy is no solution, it never has been, and the ills do not justify ripping it off. If the biblical doctrine of sin is true in any meaningful sense, no matter how you want to describe it, man is a responsible being, and his sin often lands him in misfortune, sometimes destructive to him alone, sometimes destructive to others.

Job's answer to his friends was that all suffering is not due to sin, as Job's suffering was not, regardless of what some commentators say. They just can't read. Some of the loveliest people I have known have suffered all kinds of misfortune through no fault of their own. I suspect that any reader will be able to think of situations where people have suffered who were fine people but who wound up in misery and pain through no fault of their own. And don't appeal to me about hidden sins. That is dishonest, spiritually akin to the ether theory of light transmission, which held that it must be there because there was no other explanation. That is game-playing with words and has no place in honest theological dialogue.

Therefore, in response to the question of whether misfortune pursues sinners, I think the answer is that sometimes it does, and sometimes it does not. Setting misfortune into our consideration of poverty and wealth, it means that poverty can be the consequence of sin, perhaps most clearly evidenced by the gambler who goes broke. But poverty can also be the consequence of circumstances beyond control, such as the unfortunate person with an IQ of 75, who cannot hold a job.

The other side of the proposition is that wealth is a product of virtue, and prosperity is the reward of the righteous. How true is it? There are too many variables to allow for a scientific, objective answer. A Ph.D. candidate might try to dream up a questionnaire, but would founder on such questions as where prosperity begins, what are the standards of being righteous, what is cause and what is effect. There are simply too many subjective value judgments to be made.

It is even hard to be objective in making broad observations. To show how hard it is, it is revealing to look at the entertainment field, both in drama and sports. Many well-known figures in this field are prosperous beyond any reasonable argument. But are they righteous? I will prudently avoid any individual analysis of anyone's righteousness here, first because I wouldn't welcome a lawsuit, and second because I would be making a judgment on inadequate evidence. But if a poll were conducted, I think it safe to say that some entertainers would be classified as being very good people, and others would be classified as moral reprobates of various kinds. In sports the prosperity would depend far more on skill; in the dramatic arts and popular entertainment, prosperity would depend on a combination of skill and that charismatic quality that sometimes can overcome the lack of skill.

Moving to less individualistic economic arenas, it is all too easy to become cynical about prosperity. Anyone who reads the news at all is painfully aware that there is a large, lucrative, organized crime organization in America, which earns tremendous amounts of money. There are regular stories about the way giant corporations enlarge profits in unethical ways, and every now and then such stories become part of the legal scene, such as the judgment a few years ago against the electrical manufacturing companies for price fixing.

Yet it will not do to be too cynical. For one thing, the misdeeds of others always make the news, goodness seldom does. There are countless numbers of people who are prosperous in large measure because they are trusted, and who could not continue in prosperity unless people continued to trust them. The wheels of justice grind slowly and not too precisely; but, strangely enough, they keep grinding away, and more than one man's prosperity has been taken away because he was unrighteous.

In short, prosperity is not always the fruit of righteousness. There are too many prosperous people who are not righteous, even by moderately permissive standards. Prosperity has more to do with talent than morality. But prosperity is not unrelated to righteousness, for in an interlocking society, where little can be done if people do not trust each other, the exercise of the basic virtues in economics gives stability and longevity to prosperity.

It seems as though, while the verse has a significant element of truth in it, it cannot be accepted as the whole truth. There is just too much evidence to the contrary. Nevertheless, to say the verse is totally wrong will not do, for there are many respects in which it is true. Righteousness does bring about prosperity in many cases. While it is not the same thing as saying that money is an unmitigated good, it sounds a very affirmative note on the subject.

*The Bible and Money*

Prov. 18:11 stands at the opposite pole from the passage in Ps. 52, when it says: "A rich man's wealth is his strong city, and like a high wall protecting him." It is hard to know whether to take this comment at face value or whether to believe it is delivered with tongue in cheek. The insight of the psalmist was that money is not much of a wall in the long run, but I think it would be asking a little too much to dovetail the spirit of the psalmist with this passage. It is a simple acknowledgment that wealth means power and protection. Howard Hughes used his immense wealth to insure his privacy. If any man ever erected walls with his wealth, Hughes was that man. It is certainly true that he was not bothered by many things that could irritate less affluent people. He could afford to rent two floors of a hotel just to keep others at a distance.

We must accept this fact as graciously as possible. Money can erect walls, it is useful in that sense. However, it is still subject to the limitations we discussed with respect to Ps. 52. Furthermore, I cannot hold back an unscholastic comment that walls keep people in as well as keeping people out. Living behind walls is usually not a good way to enhance our humanity.

There is an abrupt switch in attitude when we come to Prov. 23:4-5: "Do not toil to acquire wealth; be wise enough to desist. When your eyes light upon it, it is gone; for suddenly it takes to itself wings, flying like an eagle towards heaven." Here is one of the strongest statements about the transitory quality of money, a far more poetic version of our own "here today, gone tomorrow." It stands in such sharp contrast to what we have previously observed in Proverbs that it is easy to question whether it is some late addition; there is no way of knowing.

But the passage is a strong warning not to toil after money, because you can lose it in a twinkling, in just the length of time it takes to lay eyes on it. There are two ways in which it can go. It can be quickly spent. What husband or wife has not had a spouse come home with some new possession that was not planned, and with a significant quantity of money gone. "But I just couldn't resist it!" is the agelong cry. We have all been there. The other way it goes we have already discussed: we use it to pursue more money, only to lose the whole amount. The gambler is the archetype here.

The passage is another version of the necessity for controlling ourselves with respect to money. Money is like soap—it slips away, and only those people who have learned how to control their impulses are able to keep their hands on it.

The themes we have already seen in Proverbs are repeated more briefly in a few other places but, because several are concentrated in chapter 28, it is helpful to note them more briefly by way of reinforcing what already has been discussed. V. 6 tells us that better is a poor man who walks in his integrity than a rich man who is perverse in his ways. Because perverse can be interpreted in a variety of ways, it may make the verse more meaningful if we take the translation of the same word from Prov. 2:15, where it is translated as crooked. The implication of the verse is that riches have a tendency to make people crooked; and given the number of passages that deal with the need to control the appetites of people with respect to money, it becomes almost automatic to think of money as corrupting. But care must be taken not to read too much into any given passage, and this verse is not a blanket condemnation of all rich men. However, it is a value judgment giving higher esteem to integrity than to riches.

One of the very earliest themes reappears in v. 8, where it says: "He who augments his wealth by interest and increase gathers it for him who is kind to the poor." The difference between increase and interest is somewhat blurred. Broadly speaking, interest is used in a monetary context, while increase often means a portion of a product, such as a portion of grain or oil. However, the distinction is not consistently held. Either way it is another reminder of the Hebrew law against taking interest from other Hebrews. Perhaps the fate of such gains is more poetic than legal, but it does confirm the traditional Hebrew concern for the poor. The enforcement of this law against interest was probably a very difficult matter, and there do not seem to be any specific provisions for what happens to the illegal interest. Certainly justice would be done if it did go to the poor.

The two final verses of Prov. 18 are 19 and 20:

> He who tills his land will have plenty of bread, but he who follows worthless pursuits will have plenty of poverty. A faithful man will abound with blessings, but he who hastens to be rich will not go unpunished.

The first verse is a confirmation of the belief that money follows good work. As is true in many cultures, there is something of a bias in the Hebrew culture toward the virtues of tilling and tending the land, as opposed to the supposedly more prevalent vices of the city. Without pushing the distinction to the point of distortion, the idea of working hard on the soil so as to achieve plenty of bread was a pleasing one. The patience required to bring the grain in, the avoidance of sharp deals, the necessity for careful work, all combine to make the money earned by farming some kind of ideal, albeit a romantic one. Money gained this way was considered good, and a man could feel comfortable enjoying it.

Immediately following is another warning about fast money. There is a natural bias in Proverbs against fast money, with the distinct feeling present that it has a dishonest quality to it. It fits well with Prov. 10:2, which says that treasures gained by wickedness do not profit. The wise men who wrote this material could not see how any money that was earned rapidly could avoid some hint of evil, if indeed there was any good in it at all. Does their feeling stand up?

The question about fast money is most vividly illustrated for us in our gambling. Gambling does not appear to have been a major problem for the Hebrews, the word does not appear in the Revised Standard Version. Interest was the fast way of making money. But we have a much faster way in gambling. A person may win, or lose, a lot of money in a very short time, the time it takes to run one horse race, or deal a hand of cards. Speed is a virtue for the true gambler as he constantly seeks a game where there is a lot of "action," which is a slang term for the speed with which money may be won or lost. I have long felt that conventional wisdom about gambling as being primarily a way to earn something for nothing is misleading. Gambling is primarily a way to earn money rapidly with a minimum of investment and in many cases, a minimum of skill. For every person who gambles at a game like bridge, which returns money very slowly and requires a very high skill level, there are 500 people who prefer to buy lottery tickets, which return money quickly and require no skill.

Is the money thus earned by gambling evil money? Leaving aside gambling conducted under the auspices of organized crime, which introduces a new dimension, the wise men of Proverbs probably would feel very dubious about money gained by gambling because it came so very rapidly. Further, they would be dubious because the person would not have invested himself in its steady earning the way a person tilling the land does. Once again, our old cliché of "easy come, easy go" would apply.

The insights of the psalmists and the wise men of Proverbs

with respect to money lead us in several directions, continuing some themes from the earlier law and introducing some new thoughts. Some of them are positive, some are negative, and we will have to hold these various points of view in mind as we come to the great prophets of Israel and examine what they had to say about money.

## For Further Thought

The issue of virtue and wealth v. poverty and sin is often debated heatedly and illustrations abound on all sides. But I think everyone should stop to ask the question of just how much these themes are related. Do the virtuous become more wealthy than the sinners? Are those in poverty the victims of their sin or are they the victims of a system? There is no good way to find a final answer, but you might be helped if you could make up lists of examples of all the possibilities of which you have personal knowledge and see where you come out.

I have given you some thoughts on gambling, but I think it is important for everyone to consider gambling in working out feelings about money. Why is gambling evil? Or, if you happen to be among those who feel it is either good, or at least morally neutral, why do you think that way? It is all too easy for people to take the opinions of others, on either side of the argument, but that is the path of least resistance and often does nothing more than preserve the past prejudices of others. Gambling has existed in most cultures of which we have any knowledge, so it is by no means an isolated human phenomenon, but is it good or bad? It may be revealing for you to adopt the method suggested previously of listing all the reasons you can find for its worth on one side and all the reasons you can see that are negative on the other side and see where you come out.

# 4
# *Money and the Prophets*

The great prophets of Israel are more honored in retrospect than they are accepted for what they might teach people today. Whenever anyone suggests to me that religion and politics do not mix, I always ask them what they do with Isaiah, Jeremiah, Amos, Hosea, and all the other prophets of Israel. When I receive the usual blank stare, which tells me that the person is blissfully unaware of the contents of the prophets, I suggest a few verses. It is a very sobering experience for many people to discover that there is such a large body of material in the Bible that is so explicitly political. If the person is reasonably open, he learns something. If he is not, then he becomes one of that not inconsiderable group whose mind is made up and does not wish to be confused with facts. Many people would find the Christian faith so much simpler without the heritage of the prophets.

But we have this heritage, and it is a great heritage with respect to our understanding of Christian ethics. It provides us with much material about how a person should live. For

*The Bible and Money*

the benefit of readers who have lost track of their Sunday school lessons on the prophets, it might be helpful to say that the prophets of Israel were a diverse handful of perceptive men who felt called upon by God to preach about the evils they saw in the society. They preached in the period from the eighth to the sixth century B.C. They predicted the destruction of the kingdom if the people did not mend their ways, and because people seldom take such pronouncements seriously, the ways were not mended, and the kingdoms fell. Some people think that the prophets were most notable for being able to foretell the future, but such a view tends to bypass their real mission. A prophet is a man who speaks for God. With the combination of perception and inspiration that marked them all, they were able to do what perceptive and inspired people are always able to do, see the long-range consequences of human activity. Such talent does indeed permit a look into the future.

It is also helpful to know their perspective. They were not part of the formal religious establishment. There were court prophets, and in some courts quite a lot of them, but they were tame. They said not what God wanted them to say, but what the rulers wanted to hear. But the great prophets of Israel, whom we say we revere, were fiery, angry men who confronted the religious establishment with the truth and were not appreciated. Few scenes in the Bible are more moving than the scene from Amos 7:10–17, where Amos and Amaziah, the high priest, were nose to nose. Amaziah wanted Amos to get out of the way, but Amos said that he was sent by God and was not going to be budged. Amos was a mere herdsman and dresser of sycamore trees, and yet his words are part of our Scripture. Amaziah was well educated and in the upper part of society, but we only know him through his confrontation with Amos.

It is interesting that the prophets did not have a whole lot to say about money. Just about a quarter of the Old Testament is devoted to the writings of the prophets, between 225 and 300 pages, depending on how your Bible has been edited. All the meaningful references to money, riches, and wealth could fit onto one page with ease. Does this fact mean that the prophets were unconcerned about money? It is not that they were unconcerned, for the passages we shall look at are anything but unconcerned; but they were much more concerned with other aspects in the life of Israel. There are implications in many passages, which are speaking on other topics, that are consistent with the tone and direction in the more explicit passages.

The first prophet for our consideration is Amos. Though he is not the first prophet in the Old Testament as it is presented in the Bible, he is one of the first in terms of dating, about the middle of the eighth century B.C. His first principal reference to money comes in Amos 2:6: "Thus says the Lord: for three transgressions of Israel, and for four, I will not revoke the punishment; because they sell the righteous for silver, and the needy for a pair of shoes." The righteous may refer to the common practice of judges taking bribes in the courts of those days, and it may also refer to the practice of selling people into slavery for nonpayment of even small debts. Either way, it represents a gross callousness on the part of the rich toward the poor. Amos felt that the rich would go to almost any length to preserve and increase their wealth, even at the expense of another person's freedom.

Was Amos being overly cynical? In one sense he was not, for he had seen such behavior many many times. There does seem to be a tendency for some, maybe many, people who have money to become insensitive to the rights of others. Recall the passage from Lev. 25:35–37 about warning people not to take advantage of a brother's poverty. Probably you, as I, can think of people who are rich who maintain a fine sensitivity to the needs and rights of others. It is always unfair to lump people into categories. Happily we do not fit so neatly. However, the perception of Amos about the tendencies of the rich is verified by many other observers of the human scene. Money is a breeding ground for callousness, not every time, but often enough so that it is a danger to be closely associated with money.

Amos waxes poetic in the next significant passage, which is found in Amos 6:4-7:

> Woe to those who lie on beds of ivory, and stretch themselves upon their couches, and eat lambs from the flock, and calves from the midst of the stall; who sing idle songs to the sound of the harp, and like David invent for themselves instruments of music; who drink wine in Bowls, and anoint themselves with the finest oils, but are not grieved over the ruin of Joseph! Therefore they shall now be the first of those to go into exile, and the revelry of those who stretch themselves shall pass away.

That is not a flattering picture of the rich, highlighted as it is by idleness, indulgence, and indifference. The Hebrew aristocracy had beautiful summer homes up in the mountains, and when the desert weather became too warm, they retired and relaxed. Perhaps Amos had seen them as he drove his herds through the mountains. They also had fine homes in the cities, where we may safely assume similar things happened, though perhaps here the men at least attended more to business. But are idleness, indulgence, and indifference natural consequences of plenty of money?

*Money and the Prophets*

While idleness always has been considered as a consequence of affluence, as evidenced by the old phrase *the idle rich*, I think considerable care must be given to this thought of Amos's. For one thing, there is as much evidence that the poor are as idle as the rich. What is a favorite topic of the rich? Talking about the people who sit around collecting welfare and doing nothing is a part of many conversations in affluent homes. Often such conversations ignore the reality that many of these people cannot find work or may not be equipped to work in the majority of the jobs that are available. At the same moment that the affluent are talking about the idleness of the poor, the poor are complaining about the rich people who sit around on their boats, play golf, or otherwise fritter away their time.

It might be well to challenge conventional wisdom at this point and ask whether perhaps idleness has less to do with money than commonly assumed. There are plenty of people who become rich and go right on working as hard as ever. Some of them do it to be richer, some do it because they like the work, some do it to prove something to someone or something. The old story about the old and rich lawyer in the New York law factory complaining about the fact that there was no one else in the office when he left late at night is duplicated again and again in our society.

There are signs in our work-oriented culture that the strength of the old Puritan work ethic may be diminishing, but all the same most males and an increasing number of females gain much of their identity from their work, whether it earns them $5,000 a year or $50,000. However, there are always a few people around who would prefer to do nothing and having money may make it possible for them to be idle in comfort. Amos saw some of them in the mountains. And without any intention of being antifemale, in that culture women were not encouraged to develop as individuals, and may have more easily lapsed into idleness. It is hard to tell. But people who are going to be idle often are as idle when poor as they are when rich. I think it wise to be cautious if we think only about money when speaking of idleness.

Indulgence has many shades of meaning, but basically it means to gratify desires. As commonly used, it has a hint of excessiveness to it, though such a hint is not necessarily part of a formal definition. The image of the wealthy drinking wine and eating tender lamb and singing, as drawn by Amos, fits the kind of vision most people have when they think of others indulging themselves. There is no question but what having lots of money enables a person to be very lavish with indulgences. If there is any drive to indulge either one's self or others, having money enables a person to be very discriminating in the kind of indulgence chosen. If someone wants to take a group of friends skiing in Austria, and he has lots of money, he charters a jet and over everyone goes. Even grouping together to charter a jet would be considered an indulgence by many. And who has read of some of the carryings on in wealthy society and not complained about people indulging themselves on a lavish scale?

As with idleness, we should be careful not to make our brush too broad. If indulgence is the gratification of desire, the person guzzling the cheapest wine is indulging himself just as much as the rich with his bottle of fine French Burgundy. Only the price is different. The rich man may rationalize that because he is drinking a fine French wine he is somehow different from the person drinking a cheap wine, but it is only a rationalization. The poor man may be more limited in his choice of indulgences, but it is amazing the ingenuity people show in selecting indulgences, regardless of economic status. The emotion that really comes to the fore here is jealousy, because the poor, and even the not-so-poor, become envious of the rich because they can afford more spectacular forms of indulgence. Certainly there is a point at which self-gratification becomes debilitating, varying from person to person; and the indulgence, whether by the rich or by the poor, was rightly seen by Amos as detrimental to human beings. Money can help the process along and, in that sense, Amos saw it as dangerous.

How tight is the relationship between money and indifference? I think, of the three human failings cited here by Amos, that indifference may be most closely linked with money. Amos saw that these affluent people were unconcerned about the ruin of Joseph, the personification of the kingdom of Judah. Amos saw so clearly that the kingdom was in deep trouble, and it frustrated him no end that these people in positions of wealth and power could not see it. We know, in retrospect, that Amos was correct in his view of what would happen. The wealthy were unconcerned, blinded to some degree by their affluence.

How does money breed indifference? The answer is very simple. The possession of money has a very strong tendency to make people comfortable; and when people are comfortable it becomes very difficult for them to be concerned about external conditions, except when their comfort is directly threatened. It is hard to be sure, but I think it reasonable to surmise that the wealthy aristocracy of Judah had some vague idea that there were powerful enemies ready to take advantage of any weaknesses in the country. Without the news media that we enjoy, or loathe, as the case may be, there was probably a lack of immediacy about these threats to the Judeans. They were comfortable on their ivory couches, the enemy was far away, there was no need to be either anxious or involved. The more money anyone has, the more insulation he has from the kinds of problems that affect those with less money. Thus, certain kinds of problems become nonexistent, and there are few things more difficult than becoming excited about a problem that does not directly touch a given individual.

However, it would be unwise and unfair to brand all the rich as indifferent. A good example is Sen. Edward Kennedy's persistent sponsorship of medical care bills. Kennedy does not have to worry about medical bills. Even a catastrophic illness would not wipe him out financially or cut back on his consumption of steak. But he has crusaded steadily on behalf of the rest of us, for whom certain kinds of medical problems could mean economic disaster. It is possible to say that he is doing it to curry favor with the electorate, and I am sure that is partially true. But he doesn't have to do it to be elected in Massachusetts, and it is quite obvious to any but the most hardened cynics that he has a deep concern in this area, which has transcended his wealth. There are others like him, which suggests that money does not always lull the rich into indifference.

Indifference can also be found among those without much money. Part of this indifference can be traced to the fact that the poor are often numbed to life's problems and live with a constant sense of powerlessness, which in turn leads to a kind of indifference. It is paradoxical that indifference can be produced both by a lot of money and by very little money, but it seems to be true. This fact suggests that there are other factors besides money that enter into indifference, one of which is the ability to enter into another man's situation and identify with his problems. There are many others.

It may seem as though I am hedging on the question of money and indifference and possibly on the question of indulgence and idleness too. One man's hedge is another man's caution. It is a complex world and, to live in it perceptively and ethically, sweeping generalizations and labels need to be avoided like the plague. It seems as though there is a fairly high correlation between money and indifference, a lesser, though existing, correlation between money, idleness, and indulgence. And if this approach appears to dilute the teachings of Amos, remember that Amos was trying to save a nation by exhortation, and perhaps I am trying to save a people by helping them think carefully about their money.

When we turn to the massive book of Isaiah, it is surprising to find little there on the subject of money. The two principal verses are found in the 16th and 61st chapters. There is some disagreement as to authorship in this section of Isaiah. Almost every scholar today accepts the fact that there are at least two Isaiahs, with the division of the book coming after the 39th chapter. There is more disagreement about whether there is another change in authorship after chapter 55.

Even if there is a change in authorship, it is strongly held that these chapters were written following the return of the Jews from the Exile in Babylon after 538 B.C. It was a time of mixed emotions. They were joyful at being able to return to Jerusalem and overwhelmed by the problems of reconstructing their society. The prophecy gives us insight into the conditions these people faced, after several decades of being prisoners in a foreign land.

Let us take the two passages together, starting with Isa. 60:5: "Then you shall see and be radiant, your heart shall thrill and rejoice; because the abundance of the sea shall be turned to you, the wealth of the nations shall come over you." The next several verses describe the kind of riches coming in terms of camels, gold, incense, and domestic animals of various kinds. Then, in Isa. 61:6, we find: ". . . you shall eat the wealth of the nations, and in their riches you shall glory." These verses introduce a new theme of being rewarded monetarily for all the problems endured, specifically here during the Exile. The larger context of these verses is significant, because they are devoted to describing the manifestations of the glory of the Lord upon his people after all their

*The Bible and Money*

troubles, and the glory of the Lord is used both in very spiritual theophonic terms and in very concrete terms. This use of glory disturbs our normal thought patterns because most people in our society would ascribe to the word *glory* a very spiritual meaning. A useful modern synonym would be radiance. The idea that the glory of God could be revealed in both spiritual and concrete ways is alien to us.

But it was not alien to the Hebrews. The glory of the Lord was a broad thing and included such manifestations as camels and gold. The idea that God might reward anyone for enduring trials and tribulations in such concrete terms is a jarring note for most Christians, save perhaps for those devotees of a few radio preachers who are not at all bashful about offering some tangible rewards in this life. Curiously such tangible rewards come after the listener has been urged to make some kind of tangible offering. But much as this religious approach makes me cringe, I have to admit that there are biblical roots for it right in the passages of Isaiah. Another such thought is found at the end of the book of Job, where God rewards Job by giving him greater wealth than ever before. Whether it is just compensation for his previous property losses, to say nothing of the death of ten children, is another matter. It is still a very large, tangible reward for patience and suffering.

It is tempting for biblical commentators to duck away from the implication of such thoughts, and I have read such comments sadly. It is so easy to avoid reality. And the reality of these passages is that there is a biblical strand that makes a close correlation between the blessings of God and material wealth. It is not a common strand, but it clearly exists. It can be spiritualized, and thus made acceptable, but it is both inaccurate and dishonest to do so. If we assume, with a little reservation, that this prophet was aware of the many teachings about the dangers of wealth in his own tradition, and that he could speak of the glory of God in tangible terms, it can only mean that he felt that there was a good side to money. Otherwise God would not manifest his blessings or his grace in such a way. If money is inherently evil, then a good God could not act in such a way. I don't want to get off into a discussion of the goodness of God at this juncture. It is a basic part of our faith, challenged seriously by such writers as Jung, who has been too easily dimissed as a religious nut, but a serious and courageous Christian ought to meet his challenge. Let us be satisfied for the purposes of ethics that God is good and cannot manifest himself in ways that are not good.

Indeed, the only serious line of thinking to counter the direction of these passages can be to say that the prophet was simply in error in perceiving how God manifests his glory. Since most writers are extremely wary, and rightly so, of calling biblical authors wrong, preferring instead to "interpret," it well may be that we need to take the meaning of these verses at face value, and include them in our evaluation of what the Bible has to say about money.

A familiar theme by now is offered us powerfully in Jer. 17:11: "Like the partridge that gathers a brood which she did not hatch, so he who gets riches, but not by right; in the midst of them they will leave him, and at his end, he will be a fool." This rural image of the partridge who steals other children has considerably less impact in our urban day than it did in its own. Jeremiah describes the tactic of the partridge who steals and then finds herself left alone. I am not sure but what the natural children of the partridge don't go off and leave mother too, but even if the zoology is not quite correct, the meaning of the story is. The man who becomes rich in illegal fashion will lose his money right in the middle of his life, and he will wind up a fool.

If it were only so! Fortunately it happens more often than is commonly thought. It is harder to hang onto illegal money than legal money. There was no Internal Revenue Service in Jeremiah's day, but there were tax collectors. However, they did not have the tools our modern system has, and in our modern system it is comforting to those who are concerned for justice to see how often illegal money becomes revealed and people punished, losing not only large sums of money but winding up in jail. The kind of crook this system catches is important too, for often it brings in the superficially respectable, who would not dream of hitting an old lady over the head and stealing her purse, but who delight in squirreling away money to which they have no right.

Even if the legal system does not catch everyone, there is a tendency for illegal money to slip away. The same lack of internal discipline and integrity that leads people to acquire money illegally also tends to make them less disciplined when they have it. Often it slips away on the gambling tables, on luxuries, or on members of the opposite sex, and at the end such people find they have nothing left.

If this were the best of all possible worlds, everyone who collected illegal money would be caught and lose it. Because it is the world it is, not everyone in such a situation gets caught. But Jeremiah's insight reflects the thinking of many of his predecessors in Israel, who were concerned with both justice and the slippery quality that money always has and reinforces these teachings in his own day.

So far, the prophecies have considered mainly the people of Israel and Judah. Likewise Ezekiel was principally concerned with Israel, but his most moving commentary on the effect of wealth comes in his oracle against Tyre, which occupies a large part of chapter 28. Here Ezekiel describes the great wealth of that trading city in lavish terms, which were probably not too much of an exaggeration at that. This Phoenician city was one of the greatest trading ports in the world for centuries, blessed as it was by a superlative harbor. It was also noted for its purple dye. In the first part of the sixth century B.C., it shared a common enemy with Israel and Babylon. Both Jerusalem and Tyre were under seige at the same time, and Ezekiel interpreted this assault as punishment for the pride of the city, which was the consequence of its great wealth.

Vs. 5-7 summarize Ezekiel's view of the situation:

> By your great wisdom in trade you have increased your wealth—therefore says the Lord God: "Because you consider yourself as wise as a god, therefore, behold, I will bring strangers upon you, the most terrible of nations; and they shall draw their swords against the beauty of your wisdom and defile your splendor.

Then, in vs. 16-17, he expands on the nature of this sin:

> In the abundance of your trade you were filled with violence, and you sinned; so I cast you down as a profane thing from the mountain of God, and the guardian cherub drove you out from the mist of the stones of fire. Your heart was proud because of your beauty; you corrupted your wisdom for the sake of your splendor. I cast you to the ground: I exposed you before kings, to feast their eyes upon you.

It is interesting to contrast these words with the line of thought found in the days of Solomon. From Solomon's point of view, the man who labored hard and intelligently rightly deserved the wealth that would come to him. Ezekiel acknowledges the wisdom of Tyre, but takes another step and points out the corrupting effect that these gains have had, namely their hearts had become proud and they became violent. The exact nature of this violence is not mentioned. The real importance of sin is the corruption of the heart. The citizens of Tyre became too proud of their money and thus deserved to be punished.

Ezekiel is the first Old Testament writer we have encountered who has specifically mentioned the sin of pride in connection with money. The pride has reached the ultimate point for these Phoenicians because they consider themselves to be as wise as gods, and if the story of the Tower of Babel means anything, it is a warning against trying to be as wise as the gods. It is true that pride is sometimes a consequence of money. There are some people who delight in bragging about their bank balances; and there are others who delight in jewels or fine paintings. When people become too proud of their money or of the fine possessions it can buy, they lose a lot of perspective. They become insensitive to the more important considerations in life and extremely vulnerable to other kinds of excesses. It is rather interesting to see how seldom this connection between pride and money is actually made in the Old Testament. Somehow I have the feeling it should appear more often than it does.

While the prophets were more concerned about politics than money, the material we have from them is very perceptive in regard to the kinds of sin that can result from affluence. While money does not always produce idleness, indulgence, indifference, pride, or lack of discipline, the prophets saw it as having those powers, and any serious theological position must include these insights. Then there is that thought from Isaiah that money can be an expression of God's glory. That is more difficult to handle, but it can be ignored only at the risk of being dishonest and incomplete.

## For Further Thought

This chapter gives us a good opportunity to think about the rich. Is there any way to verify whether Amos was right about the rich? Or was he simply too extreme in his accusations? Another set of questions arises as to the psychological and eventually the moral differences, if any, between the rich and the poor. How do you react to the comment that a rich person is simply a poor person with more money? Or do personality changes actually take place when a person moves from poverty to riches?

A very different question arises in connection with the relevance of the words of the prophets to the present day. (I have already referred to the fact that we are often not ready to jump on prophetic bandwagons.) Do these ancient figures have any relevance for how we deal with our money? After all, it could be argued that these men were products of a very different kind of society than ours and were dealing with a far different economic situation, when there was only a handful of rich people, but there were many who were not starving, but were decidedly poor. Can the prophets speak effectively to our middle-class world? See how many objective reasons you can find to back up your feelings.

# 5
# *Jesus' Teaching about Money*

One of the first questions a Christian asks when he is faced with an ethical problem is what Jesus taught. All Christians at least give lip service to wanting to model their lives after their Lord, and a few make a great effort to do so sincerely. Only the most jaundiced of non-Christians would say that the model of Jesus was a bad example to follow. Many non-Christians, while not willing to profess a belief in Christ's divinity, in any context, greatly admire his life and accept many of his ethical teachings.

So it is crucial to study what Jesus had to say about money. In the mind of the average Christian one sentence from Jesus is worth a thousand sentences from the Old Testament, and even though such a balance may not be appropriate, the words of Jesus carry great weight. They should, for this man so fully imbued with the Spirit of God had the most profound insight into the true nature of the God–man relationship imaginable. He also knew precisely those things that hindered man from entering into the kind of relationship with God that would save him from aimlessness and sin and give him a rich and complete life.

But when we turn to the teachings of Jesus on the subject of money, we do not find very much material. In a way, this fact is surprising. Why did Jesus not devote more time to teaching about the place of this very important aspect of life? There seem to be three strong reasons.

First, Jesus was not primarily a teacher of ethics. Jesus did not analyze the problems of life and systematically set forth the way people should behave in a variety of situations. Much of his ethical teaching is not very clear. When he said, "Render therefor to Caesar the things that are Caesar's and to God the things that are God's," he was dealing with man's relation to the state, but in a way that has elicited a variety of interpretations as to exactly what he meant. It is true that he generally supported the Jewish law, which has much ethical teaching in it; but it is also true that in some places he called for more than the law required and in other places, such as when he violated the Sabbath laws, he treated them as not being too important. It would not be accurate to say that Jesus was not concerned with ethics, but I think it would be accurate to say that they were of secondary concern.

Our second point is that he was concerned primarily with how the individual was going to enter the Kingdom of God. His basic instructions to his disciples were to tell the people that they should repent, for the Kingdom of God was at hand. Precisely what he meant by the Kingdom of God has been hotly debated ever since. Some extremists take the view that the Kingdom will be here on earth; others take the view that it will be a posthistorical, otherworldly enterprise; still others believe that it is a state of the human heart. More moderate interpreters have tried to synthesize these views in various proportions. So far, after 2,000 years, no one view has proved totally persuasive, and I am not equipped to offer a final judgment on the matter, save to say that the weight of evidence in the New Testament seems to me to lean in the direction of the posthistorical, otherworldly, with some connections to human existence.

The ethics Jesus taught were primarily taught in connection with the Kingdom of God. People were not to be good for the sake of being good (too philosophical), not to be good because it made the world a better place to live (too practical), but were to be good so that they could enter the Kingdom of God. Perhaps the most powerful example of this approach is the much-loved Beatitudes, which promise rewards and punishments right straight through, with the rewards focused around the Kingdom of God and the punishments around hell. Some cynics have referred to the teaching of Jesus as being the best example of enlightened self-interest in all of religion, which seems to go too far. At the same time, any serious student of Jesus must accept the fact that he was deeply concerned with what the individual must do on his own behalf. Try, for instance, to find passages that *teach* how you can help others enter the Kingdom of God.

These thoughts lead to the third point, which is that Jesus expected the Kingdom of God to come relatively soon. Mark 9:1ff says, "Truly I say to you, there are some standing here who will not taste death before they see the Kingdom of God come with power." The same theme in connection with the teachings of the disciples is given in Matt. 10:23. Jesus further conveyed a sense of urgency to his disciples by telling them that if men didn't listen, they should shake off the dust on their feet and head for the next house or town. It would be pleasanter in Sodom on Judgment Day than in that town. There was no time to cultivate people and lead them to the Kingdom gradually, no time to set up churches where those anticipating the Kingdom could gather for mutual support and instruction.

The one theologian who tried to develop the ethical significance of this aspect of Jesus' teaching was Albert Schweitzer in *The Idea of the Kingdom of God in the Course of the Transformation of the Eschatological Faith into an Uneschatological One*, as well as in *The Quest of the Historical Jesus*. Schweitzer believed that Jesus designed his ethics for an interim period before the coming of the Kingdom, in which he demanded a kind of rigor it would be impossible to sustain over a long period, and which ignored the structural problems of a long-term society. Perhaps Schweitzer's work was not as rigorous as it should have been. Critics have attacked him severely for this thesis. But perhaps these critics have been so vehement because they felt on the defensive. What seem to be such glaring omissions in the teaching of Jesus with respect to ethics, particularly of corporate ethics, are easily explained by the "interim ethics" thesis.

Likewise, the removal of critical distinctions between feeling and action are more easily understood. If the feeling of lust and the act of adultery are equally serious sins (Matt. 5:27–28), then a person might just as well act out such an impulse. He can't be any worse off in terms of his punishment. I know such a thought is radical, but it is a perfectly logical conclusion from the Sermon on the Mount. I would quickly add that Jesus probably would have made a distinction, if pressed, but the fact that he did not, in the remembered course of his teaching, is significant.

Like most Christians, I am not comfortable with Schweitzer here. The idea that Jesus was not teaching with the long view of humanity in mind is not easy to accept. As many critics have noted, to accept Schweitzer's view of ethics would be to accept the fact that Jesus was wrong about

*The Bible and Money*

the timing of the end of history, and most Christians simply cannot tolerate the thought of a Jesus who could be wrong in any respect. Some pretty fancy interpretations have been created to explain this problem away, some persuasive, some not so persuasive. Most Christians are blissfully unaware of this problem, anyway.

But these three reasons at least give us some strong hints as to why Jesus did not devote more time to the subject of money, as well as to many subjects, as he might have. If he was not primarily concerned with ethics, it is little wonder he did not speak on the subject, just as he did not speak on war, abortion, education, and politics in a systematic way. What we really have on ethical subjects are fragments, extremely important fragments to be sure, but fragments all the same. Being concerned with the Kingdom of God, he would be less concerned with the topic of money, save for the problems it might present to a person wishing to enter the Kingdom. And if he felt in any degree that the end of history was within a generation, his interest in long-term social problems would certainly be minimal. Other things would be more pressing, and the record strongly indicates that they were.

With these thoughts as background, we can now consider what Jesus said on the subject. When I was compiling these teachings, I was trying to find some logical order in which to present them, but because the teachings are not part of a progressive series, there is no logical sequence. We will tie them up when we are done.

A good place to start is with his instructions to his disciples as offered in Matt. 10:8–10: "You received without pay, give without pay. Take no gold, nor silver, nor copper in your belts, no bag for your journey, nor two tunics, nor sandals, nor a staff, for the laborer deserves his food." This instruction is one of several where Jesus adopts a very casual attitude toward money, and here he adopts it not only on his

## Jesus' Teaching about Money

own behalf, but also on behalf of the disciples. It would appear as though Jesus made some interesting assumptions on behalf of his disciples. He assumed that the righteous in any village would shelter them and provide them with food because what they were doing was so important. Granted that hospitality to strangers was part of the social system, Jesus was still casual in his organization.

But what counted was speed, the ability to get the message spread as fast as possible. It seems reasonable to assume that Jesus was not interested in going through committee procedures and getting into a lot of planning. There was certainly no sign, here or anywhere else in his ministry, that he was organizing for the long pull. Therefore money was not an important issue. And for the length of time during which the disciples went out, his approach probably worked—at least we have no record of any problem in this respect.

But it is interesting to deal with the idea that if you receive without pay, you give without pay, especially if you are a minister, or even a layman, in a church with any concern at all for the Christian ministry. Jesus was emphasizing that because the grace of God had come upon them freely and led them to this ministry, they should go out and serve without pay. There seemed to have been no argument on the subject, and I suspect that in the presence of Jesus the question never really arose. They were men on fire. They, too, shared a sense of urgency. And so they went as Jesus commanded and literally worked their way from town to town, depending on the grace of God to feed and shelter them. And we have to take careful note that Jesus did not consider their work valueless in terms of reward, for they were to receive their food.

I have been deeply involved with the upgrading of ministerial salaries for a number of years, to the point where I have been at the helm in preparing several salary booklets and have helped to create a fund to fill the gap caused by the parsonage system. The ministry is caught between the sense of being a highly skilled, professionally oriented group, worth between double and triple what most ministers make, and an utterly selfless group who, if they are to follow this teaching as it was intended for the disciples, should serve without any pay at all. And I think many ministers in their more sensitive moments feel this conflict at a personal level. To be in a profession where the skills are equal to those of a college teacher, a middle-management executive, or a psychologist, and to receive less than a sanitation worker in New York earns, is frustrating in a society that has an interesting link between status and income. At the same time, to be aware of receiving God's calling to spread the good news as a free gift and recalling Christ's command to serve without pay puts ministers into conflict. It also puts church people into conflict.

Regretfully, there is no easy resolution to this conflict. To say that Jesus was not speaking to an organized church with a professional ministry, and therefore that this teaching does not apply, is true factually, but it certainly violates the spirit. To say that the laborer is worthy of his food can be expanded into including shelter, clothing, and transportation without too much stretching, but how much stretching can you expect to make the verse take when you want a vacation in Europe? It is an interesting problem and bears a relationship to the problems of the religious institution supporting itself, which we saw in the Old Testament law.

Further evidence of Jesus' casualness about money is to be found in that well-known section in the Sermon on the Mount (Matt. 6:25–34) where Jesus tells his listeners that they should not be anxious about food and clothing, citing the evidence of the birds and lilies of the field. The story is also given to us in Luke, so it is highly likely that this teaching is

## Jesus' Teaching about Money

genuine. It does not specifically mention money, but it so clearly relates to the economic activity of the world with respect to earning, saving, and planning that to bypass it would be totally dishonest.

So much attention has been given to this teaching, and so many interpretations have found their way into books and sermons that it is difficult to say something new about it. The principal point of the teaching seems to be that if anyone trusts deeply in the Lord God Almighty with a kind of joyous abandon, there won't be any need to worry about some of these basic necessities of life. Jesus conducted his ministry with that kind of faith, moving from town to town, picking corn along the way, even on the Sabbath. Somehow, someone always provided Jesus and his followers with food and shelter or, to be more accurate, we never read of them starving. Maybe they did from time to time, and it certainly would not be easy for a Gospel writer to report it.

In thinking about the joyous free trust that Jesus had, it may be worthwhile to remember that, as far as we can tell, Jesus had been a regular carpenter, probably with his father at first and then, after his father died, continuing on in that trade until he was called to his ministry. Even in those simpler days carpentry was a skilled trade, which required the ability to plan. The family had many mouths to feed and, particularly after Joseph died, Jesus must have had the major responsibility of supporting his family. He made chairs and tables so that there would be bread on the table and clothes on the younger children. To be sure, they did not enjoy a high standard of living by present western world standards, but a skilled tradesman would not be on the bottom of the economic pile even in first-century Israel.

As we have done before, we can question how true this teaching is. If we don't take thought for the coming days and years, will God provide the basic necessities of life? The kind of backing and filling done by some commentators is wondrous to behold. George Butterick, who is one of the most gifted preachers of this or any other century, said in his commentary on Matthew in the *Interpreter's Bible* (Nashville: Abingdon Press, vol. 7, p. 321): "Second, it is a fair assumption that God, having given the great gift of life, will not provide for its temporal needs.... Third, there is ample evidence of this kindly providence. The birds are fed, the flowers clothed, and even the grass is sustained in its proper life. These 'creatures' all fulfill their nature, and God provides for them. If man fulfills his nature (not idleness, but trustful work) God does not fail him, even though death should come." This kind of romantic interpretation strongly implies that God provides, even though Butterick covers himself with his parenthetical comment about trustful work.

I know enough about birds to know that birds have to work continuously in order to get enough to eat, and that sometimes they starve in winter. And the sight of burned lawns reminds me that even the grass does not always make it. Starving millions in India and elsewhere remind us that when work is not available, and often even when it is, there is not enough food in many parts of this world to feed those who need it. Nor is it reasonable to say that if all those millions of starving Hindus became Christians, they would find food on their table. God does not automatically provide the necessities of life. It takes planning; and on this planet, with its rapidly increasing population, it is going to take a lot more planning than most people are presently doing to provide enough food, let alone the other necessities of life. The teaching of Jesus here is just simply not true in a practical sense, even though we can affirm that we must not let the need for planning the future in so many ways become an idol.

I believe this teaching of Jesus is an example of the tension we face, between the requirements laid down for the entrance into the Kingdom of God by Jesus and the need for enough money to meet our needs over a long period of time. A ghetto dweller, who can neither find work nor grow his own vegetables, is not going to feel much like not worrying about food for tomorrow, for he knows full well that the grocer will want cash at the check-out counter. The ghetto dweller may want to enter the Kingdom of God, but he also wants to eat. To what extent Jesus' belief that the Kingdom was coming soon colored this teaching it is hard to tell, but certainly it is much easier to accept this attitude if you do not need to worry about the distant future. I suspect that only those who visualize a short future can assume the attitude called for by Jesus; for the rest, there is the need to plan economically so that responsibilities can be met, especially in our completely interdependent society, where so many people are totally removed from the land.

Also in the Sermon on the Mount, Jesus recalls the spirit of some Old Testament passages when he says in Matt. 6:19–21: "Do not lay up for yourselves treasures on earth where moth and rust consume, and where thieves break in and steal, but lay up treasures in heaven."

Here, once again, is the theme of the slippery nature of money. Most people react with surprise to moths in this verse, but they attack clothes and rugs with a vengeance, and in a society where proportionately more value was found in such items, and moth-proofing was not available, the loss could be quite substantial. Rust is not a perfect translation of the Greek, but it will serve us well enough if we consider what damage rust would do to iron tools that did not have the benefit of the rustproofing available today. Then, as now, thieves were a perpetual problem, and a person could build up substantial wealth, only to have it stolen in a few minutes.

By contrast the treasures of Heaven were far more enduring in the mind of Jesus. Treasure, in this context, is clearly a poetic word, as there is not the slightest evidence that Jesus conceived of Heaven as a place where there would be monetary riches, such as gold or jewels. Those who want to take the dazzling description of the holy city in Revelation literally and as refuting this point may do so, and there is no objective argument possible. But everything I see in the Gospels indicates that the virtue of Heaven is not jasper walls and gold streets, but the nearer vital presence of God and the company of the elect who have accepted God's offering. The Kingdom of God is always going to be there. It is fixed in the mind of God, and cannot be destroyed by any natural or human force.

The passage also shows how clearly Jesus saw the attraction of money. He knew what every preacher knows, that if you can persuade a person to put some money into a project that person is going to become very interested in and will often develop a strong loyalty to it. A person concerned with getting and defending wealth from moths, rust, and thieves is not going to pay much attention to the Kingdom of God. This feeling of Jesus moves away from just being casual about money to the position that money, besides being slippery, is a negative factor in man's religious pilgrimage.

In Luke 18:19-25, Jesus becomes much more specific in the story of the man who came to him and asked him what he had to do to inherit eternal life. Jesus recited some familiar commandments and then told him to sell everything he had and give the proceeds to the poor. That was more than the man could handle, and he backed away fast. Jesus then turned to his disciples, probably sadly, and said those well-known words, "It will be easier for a camel to go through the eye of a needle than for a rich man to enter the Kingdom of God."

Jesus did not say it was impossible to enter the Kingdom of God. Jesus loved both Nicodemus and Zacchaeus. But the

*Jesus' Teaching about Money*

very hyperbole in this illustration is a clear indication that he viewed riches as a very serious barrier to the Kingdom of God. There are those who argue that the illustration means that it is impossible. After all, there are no camels who could fit through even the largest eye of the largest needle and the stretched interpretations, which try to translate the eye as being the wicket gate in a large door and the camel as rope, are not acceptable to the majority of scholars.

It is a hard teaching, and even the disciples were amazed. They knew the teachings we have examined, and how much support there was for wealth in the Old Testament. The fact that interpreters have tried to circumvent the meaning of the words with stretched translations indicates the resistance we continue to show even to the present day. The only thing that keeps the story from being a flat prohibition is the story of Zacchaeus, (Luke 19:1–10) who actually repented his misusing of money and received the assurance of Jesus that salvation had come to his house. However, to achieve it, he gave half his goods to the poor, and restored four times as much to those he had defrauded. Salvation did not come to him while he had his original fortune, he had to repent and make appropriate restoration.

Some uncomfortable preachers, perhaps those who receive top salaries in their profession, have raised the issue of what is truly rich, pointing out that Jesus did not bother to define a rich man. If only J. Paul Getty, Nelson Rockefeller, and a few other tycoons are rich, then we can commiserate with them on their misfortune in being so filthy rich, but those with less than, say, $100 million in assets do not need to worry.

Such sophistry would do credit to some of the ancient Pharisees. It is true that the definition of a rich man is partially subjective and depends a lot on where you live. It is interesting how many people with substantial incomes, which put them in the top percentage, do not feel that they are rich.

*The Bible and Money*

Ask any lawyer who earns $50,000 a year whether he is rich, and virtually all will answer no. For them, someone who is rich is like Dr. Jones down the street, who rakes in $125,000 delivering babies. But when you go down the street to Dr. Jones, he is not likely to admit he is rich either, and points to someone in industry making $200,000 and holding a piece of the company as being rich. On the other end of the scale, there is the ancient pulpit appeal for mission money because those in foreign countries are so very very poor that all the people in the church are very rich by comparison. There is no avoiding the fact that a person with a pension, Social Security, and $4,000 or $5,000 in annual income would be considered very rich in India or Indonesia, even though they feel rather poor here.

Is there any objective definition of a rich man by which we may measure the teaching of Jesus and some of the Old Testament, too? I would propose one, with the full knowledge that there are a lot of flaws in it. A person is rich when he or she has sufficient income to purchase the necessities of life and still has enough left over to purchase goods and/or services that are not necessities.

There are several vulnerable words in that definition. Necessity is by no means unambiguous. Food, clothing, and shelter are the three traditional basic necessities. But even here there is room for question. How much food of what kind is debatable. Is the necessity for shelter met when four children must sleep together in one room? We could digress endlessly on the basics alone. Then there are other problems, such as a car, a TV set, a telephone, medical care—you good readers could quadruple the list in short order. There are many things the majority of Americans consider necessities today that were luxuries (or nonexistent) thirty years ago.

There is room for debate over what would constitute a discretionary income, made more difficult by what seems to

## Jesus' Teaching about Money

me to be unarguable, that there is no one single dividing line between necessary and discretionary income. Obviously, to me, anyway, a person who puts silver-plated plumbing fixtures in his bathroom has a discretionary income. A person who takes a summer vacation in Europe each year has a discretionary income. But does the person who buys a medium-size Buick have a discretionary income? He could buy an Apollo for his automotive necessity. The fact remains that there comes a point in the lives of a number of Americans when they are able to make relatively free choices about how they will spend their money, and I think it is at this point that they can be considered rich by biblical standards. As to what that annual dollar figure is, I would surmise that, at the moment, it is between $15,000 and $25,000 for a small family, depending on which subculture they inhabit. I can see the rising wrath of those making $15,000 a year who still feel pinched, but I still say that those people have choices about how they spend some of their money.

I think the above definition is useful because, at the point where people can begin to exercise free choice over how their money is spent, the chance rapidly increases that money will become an idol and, as an idol, have power to corrupt by focusing a disproportionate amount of attention on the money itself, or on what it can buy. It seems a reasonable conclusion, from reading the teachings of Jesus, that when anything at all distracts a person from doing what is needed to enter the Kingdom of God, Jesus speaks powerfully against it. For Jesus, the problem of the rich man is not his riches per se, but their diverting and distracting influence. Therefore, it seems reasonable to conclude that the biblical definition of *rich* begins at the point when people have some freedom to spend, over and beyond the necessities of life. It is a freedom we all would like to enjoy, and our American dream is to climb to that point, in spite of Jesus' teaching. For most people, comfort and freedom of choice is more important than entering the Kingdom of God.

One of Jesus' parables, which has given comfort to those who would seek justification for riches, is that of the talents (Matt. 25:14-30 and Luke 19:12-28). For those who have forgotten, a man calls his three servants as he is about to take a trip and gives them each some money: one about $5,000, one about $2,000, and the last about $1,000. The two who had the larger sums went out and doubled their money. The poor fellow with just $1,000 turned nervous, hid it in the ground, and returned the original sum. The master was angry. He told the servant he should, at the very least, have put it in the bank, took it away from him, gave it to the man who now held $10,000, and threw the coward out.

There have been those throughout the ages who have used this story as an illustration that Jesus was not really against money and expected people to expand what they had. Such interpreters take the talent at its face value of being coin of the realm, worth about $1,000 in our terms, and say that Jesus looked upon these transactions with obvious approval.

It is always interesting to see how obvious parables are to people, and how two very different meanings can seem obvious to two different people. Those of you who are familiar with theological writing know that the time to be most careful of an author's argument is when he precedes it with the magic words "It is clear" or "It is obvious." More often than not it means that the author is convinced, and honestly so, that he is right, but has little or no objective data to back him up. However, I would argue here that, because the parable is in conflict with the rest of Jesus' teaching on the subject, the parable is not about money at all: It is about the free and courageous use of all that God has given us. It is pure coincidence that the sum of money involved is called a talent, but it makes it easy for preachers to call for full use of all the talents that a person has. Money is the medium of the illustration, but it is not the real point of the parable.

Perhaps it would be helpful to summarize our discoveries with a few comments to tie up a few of the loose ends. Jesus taught his disciples to venture forth with more faith than money, with the implication, if not the full command, that those who would follow him should not worry about money. He taught a casualness toward money, with the implication that God will provide for those who are faithful, which can be debated on the grounds of reality. And he looked on money as a corrupting influence in the lives of people, which represented a major obstacle to entrance into the Kingdom of God.

These are not happy teachings for our twentieth-century western civilization (not to mention the oil shieks of the Near East). They put an enormous strain on those in the religious establishment, who want to take the teaching of Jesus seriously and faithfully, yet must live in a world where money is present in unprecedented quantities. Is there no hope for the middle-class American because of this situation? Most people don't worry about it much. In fact, they worry about how to get more money even when they have substantial freedom of choice, and they look at Jesus in this context simply as being impractical. In our society you can largely ignore what is impractical.

One interesting point is that, in spite of all Jesus taught, he never specifically said that money is bad in and of itself. He was concerned about what it did to people. I realize it is a fine point, yet I feel it has to be made, because there have been a few people who have taught that Jesus felt money was evil, bad, and wicked. It is just not true. Jesus knew that it was not the things outside a man that corrupted him, but the things inside, and money falls into the outside category. If we must deal with this difficult problem, let us at least deal with

*The Bible and Money*

it accurately. However, the other material in the New Testament is considered by some, if not all, to be equal in authority to the Gospels, so let us turn our attention to other New Testament teachings before we come to any final conclusions.

## *For Further Thought*

I doubt that anyone has raised a totally new question about the teachings of Jesus in centuries, so I will not pretend to do so here. But some questions look different in different contexts, and it may prove helpful to go over some old ground in these new contexts.

One interesting thing to test would be what a group of people think constitutes a rich person. Two points of procedure will be helpful. The first point is to have each person in the group do so without telling the others. Otherwise you will be into an argument before two people have finished, which could have a surprising influence on the rest of the group. The second point is to make sure that each person is working from the same assumptions. Don't ask "How rich is rich?" Ask them to say how much income a person should have in order to be considered rich, or what amount of investments in a total holding of land, stocks, and other tangible assets is needed. For those who are unfamiliar with capital assets, the income approach is probably easier.

Once you have found out where people begin in their thinking, you can work toward a common definition, and then you can test it against the teachings of Jesus. At what point would money become a barrier to entering the kingdom of God? I think to wrestle with this thought, which is the basis of Jesus' own teaching, would be most instructive for Christians. For non-Christians it is not so much of a problem, but they can still profitably raise the question: At what level does money become a temptation—from their own definitions of the good life?

The other question that needs clarification for so many people is: How rigorous did Jesus intend people to be in following his ethical teachings? Did he really give us an impossible mission and if so on what basis, biblical and otherwise, can we make modifications? Most people make a lot of modifications, and it is helpful to get these out in the open and examine them.

# 6
# *The Rest of the New Testament*

I wish there was some way to handle the other New Testament books in a systematic fashion, but, once again, the fragmentary nature of our subject makes it impossible. The average reader loses sight of the fact that each New Testament book was written on its own terms with its individual concerns and was not designed to be part of a larger work. The amount of material rejected by the early church as being unworthy of inclusion in an official canon was very great. If it had all been accepted as authoritative, the New Testament would be more than twice as big as it now is.

When it came to money, the authors spoke of it when they saw a need to teach something to their readers. The majority of the New Testament books are letters written to instruct some part of the community of faith on some aspect of the Christian life and, more often than not, to solve problems that had arisen. Curiously enough, the two largest books in the non-Gospel section of the New Testament are not letters. Acts is part of the Gospel of Luke, the separation in our edi-

## The Rest of the New Testament

tions being to put the four Gospels together. Revelation was a treatise to persecuted Christians undergoing the savage attack of Rome but goes far beyond the dimensions of a mere letter.

Money, seemingly, was not a major problem in the life of the early church. First of all, it didn't have much, and second, the problems of what to believe and how to behave with respect to each other and to outsiders were far more pressing than the issues of money.

Some may wonder whether there is enough data in the whole Bible to put together a coherent theology of money. After all, it could be argued that there have been very few passages. But theological conclusions have been drawn at length from just one or two passages, sometimes at very great length. I think we will see, by the end of this chapter, that some of the themes we have seen before are once again offered us and will provide us with enough data for some conclusions.

The book of Acts gives us two interesting passages about money, the first being the story of Ananias and Sapphira (Acts 4:32-5:11). In that first community of the faithful, after Jesus rose, those at its core held property in common and provided for the necessities of life. Ananias and Sapphira sold some property, but held out a portion of the proceeds from the community. Such secrets were just as hard to keep then as they are now, and when Peter discovered it and confronted Ananias with it, Ananias went into some kind of shock and died, followed shortly by his wife. There has been speculation that they were executed, but there is no evidence for such a conclusion, and the spontaneous death of the couple says much more about the price of sin.

We are more interested in what the story has to say about money. It describes an economic structure within the life of the early church. It was a structure born out of love and concern that no one would suffer and I suspect, in some part, to keep the more affluent from dominating the situation. Some people have called it communism, which must make Marx roll over in his grave. It was not the ownership by the state of the means of production. It was an experiment in communal living. The money was under the control of the group, which is another example of the need to control people and their money.

Ananias and Sapphira are an example of what happens when a person loses the right kind of control over money. Ananias wanted to be seen by the community as generous, but he could not bring himself to let go of the whole sum. Perhaps, in the sale of the property, which may have been a house or a piece of land, he suddenly had found himself with more cash than he had ever seen. That kind of temptation overcame his commitment to share fully with the group.

Apparently that community did not maintain itself in that form for too long. We have passages in some of Paul's letters that reveal offerings taken for the church in Jerusalem, and we will deal with those shortly. But the communal church could not endure. Ever since then many groups have tried to live in that style, but the vast majority of them find it difficult to maintain. There is something beautiful about the attempt, and in principle it seems so right in traditional Christian terms. But the economics of the situation is so often a hindrance that such groups find it very hard to endure.

Another problem for that community in Acts was that it lived in immediate expectation of the Parousia. The early zeal and expectations could sustain the rather crude economic arrangements. But when the second coming did not come, it seems reasonable to assume that this life-style began to unravel. They were not equipped structurally to operate over a long period of time, and psychologically it would have been difficult for them to remain close when the original expectation of Jesus' return did not come to pass.

To conclude our thoughts on this passage, it is significant to note that there is no suggestion by Peter that there was anything inherently wrong with the couple owning property or selling it for the benefit of the community. It was a tacit acknowledgment by Peter that the community needed economic support. What the community could not stand, as is true of all close communities, is a cheat. When trust is lost, things come unglued fast. The lure of an extra piece of change proved too much for them to withstand. It is a sad story, because it shows so well how easy it is for money to get in the way of a holy commitment.

We saw in the previous chapter that Jesus taught his disciples that they should serve without pay, because God had freely given them so much. The disciples took this teaching to heart, if the story of Simon (Acts 8:18-20) is to be believed. Simon wanted to buy the power of the Holy Spirit from the disciples. Peter took a long look at this man. We know about Simon from extra-biblical sources, and it seems probable that he was the leader of a religious sect that tried to rival Christianity. The sources are highly biased, and it is quite impossible to tell whether he was an outright charlatan or a devout man who believed sincerely in what he was preaching. Peter was not impressed, he felt the man bitter and bound by sin, and told him that he would perish along with his silver because he thought he could obtain the gift of God with money. The Holy Spirit was not for sale, indeed it could not ever be sold.

The story is significant because it reveals another insight about money. There is a tendency to believe that money will buy anything. The old clichés such as "money can't buy happiness" or "money can't buy love" exist because someone is always trying to purchase things with money that simply cannot be bought. There are few who do not occasionally feel that they can. Try suggesting to a friend that money cannot buy happiness and discover how often the response will be that he or she wouldn't mind trying. Point out that Ted Kennedy has had a history that would make most people miserable, and a common reaction is that his money cushions the pain.

Another aspect of this problem is seen in the political sphere, where one theory on the way to improve the world is to spend more money. Labels are misleading, but this view usually has been associated with what is generally considered the liberal side of politics. The problems of the country would be solved if we would just spend more money in certain areas. This is another version of money buying happiness—along with some votes. Such an approach meets sharp opposition from those who believe in the virtues of austerity and draw much support from some versions of Christianity, which herald the virtues of being poor.

It does not become the Christian to be too self-righteous on this point. People who laud the virtues of austerity, in the political arena particularly, and piously remind others that happiness cannot be purchased, very seldom live on an inadequate diet themselves, or have to contend with cold running water and hot running cockroaches. There is a connection between happiness and money, perhaps more so in our society, where the percentage of poor is relatively low in comparison to most other countries of the world today, and of virtually all societies in past history. No one I know is in a rush to become poor just so that he can be happy.

There is even some irony connected with some of the modern experiments in communal living, where people are trying to get away from the rat race of accumulating possessions. I visited such a place once. There was a lot of austerity present: very simple beds, a vegetable garden outside, old clothes on everyone. They were trying However, I noticed five single-lense reflex cameras and a lovely sound system. Maybe I should have pointed out such incongruities, but I just couldn't, probably because I like music and photography myself. Money can make me happy at one point in my life—when I am listening to full rich sound. Peter was undoubtedly right in rebuking Simon. He was trying to purchase the grace of God, which is a truly free gift, and he had missed the point. But we shouldn't be too hard on him—there is a lot of Simon in most of us.

Paul was a dynamic influence in the church as evangelist, teacher, and problem solver. I have always been amazed at the breadth of his ministry. Some critics have accused him of taking a simple faith and making a complex theology out of it, but such critics fail to remember first, that it was by no means a simple faith, and second, that if Paul had not done it, someone else would have. No religion endures for long without some kind of intellectual formulation, even though that formulation sometimes seems to take on a life of its own. The difficulty of that task is seen to be all the greater when those of us with the perspective of two thousand years of experience realize that Paul had to interpret the faith with very little upon which to draw. Can you imagine trying to interpret the faith to new churches without being able to refer to the four Gospels?

Paul did not leave us any specific teaching about money, but some of his activity in the churches had a financial aspect that should be considered. We saw in the second chapter how the Jewish law provided for the support of the religious institution. Now the theme appears in the life of the new institution, centered around the church in Jerusalem. The circumstances are not absolutely clear, but there are enough references in the letters of Paul to demonstrate that the church in Jerusalem needed help. It is not known whether this money was to support the institution or to take care of the needs of the poor, perhaps both. The references are to "the poor," which implies that individuals were the primary concern. There are brief references to this situation in Rom. 15:25–28, 1 Cor. 16:1–3, 2 Cor. 8:1–9,15, Gal. 2:10, and Phil. 4:14–18.

By far the longest of these references is the passage in 2 Cor., which occupies two full chapters. There is still virtually no information about the Jerusalem church, but the chapters are a fine example of how to raise money for worthy causes. Paul describes how generous the Macedonians have been, in spite of being poor. The Macedonians did not wait to be asked to help the church in Jerusalem, they volunteered to relieve the plight of the saints. A saint was a person consecrated to God, which could apply to any Christian and usually did not have the overtones that Christian history has given it. However, we could reasonably assume that the members of the Jerusalem church would have enjoyed some eminence as those who had been in the city where Jesus died and who had inspired the first church. It made the appeal for money more persuasive, and Paul needed every advantage he could get with the stubborn Corinthians.

Paul's appeal was based on the generosity of Christ himself. Jesus had been rich, not in earthly wealth, but in his preexistent state. But he became poor so that other people, specifically the Corinthians, might be rich. That model has been used in many forms by the church ever since. Jesus is the ultimate example of generosity and sacrifice for the Christian, and the members of his church are asked to pattern themselves after him. I suppose a real spoilsport would want to know when Christ ever gave money to anyone, which is never as far as our records are concerned. The point is that he gave his life so that we might have life, and nothing could be more generous than that. Money is to be shared with those who are in need.

Paul had another angle to his pitch, which has something of the tone of some of Solomon's and Isaiah's teachings. 2 Cor. 9:7-8 reads: "... for God loves a cheerful giver. And God is able to provide you with every blessing in abundance, so that you may always have enough of everything in abundance for every good work." The giver is not to go unrewarded for his generosity, and that reward is not only spiritual, but material. The spirit is similar to that of Jesus in the Sermon on the Mount, where he promises over and over again that there shall be powerful spiritual rewards for those who follow the right path, though Jesus never promises material rewards. The material rewards cited by Paul are not to be used selfishly for individual pleasure. They are to be used for "every good work," which means carrying out the kind of ministry Jesus did.

What can we deduce about money from these passages? First, and most important, money is a means of expressing generosity in a concrete way, i.e., 2 Cor. 8:8: "... but to prove by the earnestness of others that your love is genuine." This theme had been very important in the life of the church. Countless offertory sentences have contained this theme. To be a Christian is to be generous, because Jesus was generous to us. Since most of us cannot, and would not, if we were honest, sacrifice our lives for others in the same literal fashion as Jesus did, we can do the same thing symbolically by sacrificing our money.

Confirmation of this theme is to be seen in the letters of John, where he makes the strong point that love must be concrete in order to be love (John 2:9-11, 3:15-17). You can't just run around saying you love people and then treat them shabbily. Money can be a means of expressing love for people. When a husband cares for a wife and children, one of the things he does is to provide a home and all that goes therein. Love can be expressed for faraway people in dire straits by sending money for their relief.

## The Bible and Money

I know that there are those who are most anxious to tell me that money is often a substitute for love. A husband may give a wife a mink coat and not provide her with the understanding attention she needs. We might give money to a disaster that occurred far away out of a sense of guilt. There are even a few people who appear to try to buy salvation in the church by generous gifts, a la Simon, the magician.

But before we expound on too many negative stories, of which there are more than enough, I think we have to acknowledge that there are a whole lot of people who have expressed their love for others in a rational and caring manner through the thoughtful use of their money. Ministers are not all cynics when they ask their congregations to express their love for God with their gifts. At the risk of being overly sentimental, I recall, many years ago, some denominational drive for capital funds. I visited an elderly widow whose health was erratic and whose living conditions were worse than erratic. She had heard me mention the drive in church, asked several intelligent questions, and then pulled $20 out of her purse. I hesitated to take it and, reading my hesitation very well, she told me that she wanted to be part of a good cause because "Isn't that what Jesus would like?" Simple, yes, but we all should be this simple. This lady knew how to use her money to show she cared.

Second, the passages in 2 Corinthians show us that money was an accepted part of the life of the church. Paul saw nothing amiss in calling on the churches he founded for support of the saints in Jerusalem. He did not try to excuse the request or, even more significant, try to spiritualize it too much; he simply told the people that there was need in Jerusalem and taught them why they should respond to the need. The Corinthians were rather more reluctant than the Macedonians and Philippians, but that should not come as a surprise. There are some congregations today more generous

*The Rest of the New Testament*

than others. In fact, I think we can take our evidence in Acts and in these letters and conclude that money was taken for granted as being an integral part of the life of the church. The church did not yet have a professional ordained clergy, massive houses of worship, or basketball teams, but even the most embryonic of human organizations very quickly gets into budget difficulties. I think we can assume that it was no different for the early church.

Another kind of problem led Paul to a comment in 2 Thess. 3:6–13, which has been used in a variety of ways ever since. The problem in Thessalonia was that there some people were hangers-on. They didn't work, they meddled in other people's affairs, and they seemed to have been a very disrupting influence as they sponged off the fellowship. Paul reminded the church that when he and his companions had been with them, they had paid for everything they had eaten, and had worked day and night so that they would not be a burden to anyone. Paul had a very simple message for these loafers: no work, no eat.

This injunction has been a two-edged sword. On the positive side, it asks that people be responsible for their own lives at the most basic point, food, and, by reasonable extension, for all the aspects of their lives. Since people do not obtain food except by growing it or buying it, it means that most people should work enough to supply their own food. It would be hard to find a passage that runs counter to human responsibility, save for those teachings of Jesus about not being anxious for the morrow, which we have already reviewed.

On the negative side, it has encouraged certain stony types to look with disdain on those who are unable to work. The line between wanting to work and being able to work grows steadily more cloudy in our society where those with minimal skills steadily lose jobs, whether through elimination of jobs or through increasing disdain for some kinds of manual and personal service jobs. One of the attractions of the recent TV series, "Upstairs, Downstairs," was its portrayal of the servant class, which we see as anachronistic, and we see it that way because almost no one is willing to work in that category today. But the net result is an increasing number of people who do not work, who in some cases cannot work, in other cases who would like to, but cannot compete in the job market. Those who view welfare roles as the depository for loafers find a lot of comfort in Paul's injunction and use it to justify allowing only the barest possible existence for such people.

What does it say about money? It says one should earn enough money to provide the basic necessities of life. It is not helpful in analyzing what constitutes a basic necessity. To earn enough not to be a burden on others is a goal desired by most people, but at what level such a state is achieved is not easy to determine. I think it reasonable to assume that Paul does not see enough danger in this level of earning power to issue warnings about the corrupting or negative side of money. Paul was very quick to speak when he saw moral danger. Presumably, anyone who earned only enough to purchase the basic necessities was in little danger of being corrupted. Paul may have been a little optimistic on that score—I have known some people on welfare to gamble at the racetrack and consume an unhealthy amount of alcohol. Determinative in Paul's teaching was the fact that, with a few notable exceptions, most of the Christians in the early church were poor people. The problems of discretionary income did not greatly affect his ministry.

It also indicates that money is a normal part of living, which is not readily abandoned. Paul did not suggest any kind of utopian society, in which money would not be necessary, and he did not suggest that members of churches needed to take vows of poverty, again, perhaps, because they were poor from the start. Paul did not have the same sense of the end of history that Jesus did. Paul did indicate in 1 Cor. 7:29-30 that this world was passing away and that people should act accordingly, but elsewhere he seems to be setting people up for a longer haul which meant that some of the normal structures of society needed to be maintained. I suspect scholars and others will argue the relative balance of these forces for many more centuries, but for our purposes we can say that Paul instinctively felt there would be enough need for a social structure so that money would be a necessary part of the scene.

When we turn to the pastoral Epistle of 1 Timothy, we discover two little pieces of information, one obsure and the other quite well known. But first, we should ask whether Paul was the real author, or whether these are the products of later years, for it makes some difference to our understanding of the money passages. The vocabulary of the author and the descriptions of the church structure strongly suggest that the author was not Paul but some unknown church leader who paid Paul the honor of writing in his name, a typical practice of the period. While the issue is still open to some doubt, the evidence persuades me that those who see the Epistles as early second century products, perhaps as much as half a century after Paul, have the correct view.

The first passage is 1 Tim. 3:3, where the author speaks about the qualities necessary to be a good bishop (that word never appears in letters attributed to Paul), including the virtue of not being a lover of money. Was this quality based on Jesus' command to his disciples not to expect money for their ministry? Or was it a more generalized kind of admonition, which looked for safe and sober virtues in the leadership of the church? Perhaps it was both, but I suspect the latter carried more weight. The disciplined Christian leader of the early second century would not be a person of excesses in any regard. There is no evidence that the bishop would need to give away all his money.

The word love appears again in 1 Tim. 6:10, where one of the most famous sayings about money appears: "For the love of money is the root of all evils; it is through this craving that some have wandered away from the faith and pierced their hearts with many fangs." It is interesting that so many people misquote the verse, omitting "the love of" and dropping the "s" from evils. The reader will particularly want to look at the verses immediately preceeding this famous one in order to set the passage in context.

Money here is not a means of expressing generosity, as Paul tried to teach his churches. It is an out-and-out peril. The peril lies not in the money itself, but in the desire for it, and the author sees this desire as the foundation of everything that is evil. Here the author has captured what Jesus had been teaching, as well as confirming what a number of other religions have taught. There are similar teachings in Stoicism and in Buddhism. The ancient Hebrews were not such extremists, as we have seen, but there were ample quotations from the Old Testament to at least point in this direction. This particular saying may have been from a proverb current at the time, representing a more exaggerated and poetic version of what was considered conventional wisdom.

How can one best deal with such an extreme statement to achieve some kind of coherent thought about money itself? Certainly there would be many who would take the statement at its face value, depending on verbal inerrancy or a close equivalent. Broad statements, which purport to identify or solve a problem in a few words, are always attractive. If it were possible to point to the love of money and place upon it the culpability of all the evil in the world, life would be so simple. We could throw all the money in the sea and, without money to love, evil would be banished to the swirling depths where it could try to attract the attention of crustaceans and codfish.

If I appear to be too cynical, it is because I do not tolerate oversimplified solutions to either questions or answers very well. I am grateful when they are possible, but they are so seldom possible that it must be better to be more discriminating and imaginative. The love of money is just not the root of all evil. When sexual desire overwhelms a man, one of the results is rape, which I hope all would agree is an evil. It does not have anything to do with money, except in those situations where robbery accompanies it, which is almost always incidental. Likewise, almost everyone would agree that murder is evil. The gangster killings that make the headlines would at first glance suggest that murder and money are deeply involved. But the far more common murders among friends, lovers, family, and even strangers often have nothing to do with money. And these two illustrations by no means exhaust the possibilities of evils.

I do not claim any special knowledge of human motivation that the author of Timothy probably did not have in much greater degree than I. Human nature has not changed that much over the centuries. Therefore, I think we need to acknowledge that he set the proverb in the context of Jesus' position on money, which was that it was very unimportant, with 1 Tim. 6-7, "For we brought nothing into the world, and we cannot take anything out of the world," showing how close he was to the feelings and teachings of Jesus. He knew objectively that money was not the root of all evils, but so clear and present a danger was it that he felt obliged to state his case as strongly as he could.

Special note needs to be taken of the fact that the author differentiates between the love of money and money itself. He was not as apocalyptically oriented as some of the earlier writers. He was part of a church that, though it believed in the second coming, did not live in sensitive anticipation of the immediate event. It will come in the "proper time" (1 Tim. 6-15). Thus there had to be a way for people to live, and money was taken for granted. There was no way to do without it.

However, the life-style of the Christian was to be austere. "But if we have food and clothing, with these we shall be content." (1 Tim. 6-8). It seems safe to assume that he would not have wanted Christians to sleep under the stars in the cold of winter, so shelter would be a legitimate assumption. In our society, the people who have only food, shelter, and clothing are considered poor and dislike their position with varying degrees of intensity. They are rarely content; and often what passes for contentment is resignation. But even if twentieth-century America does not like such austerity, it is very difficult to rationalize this paragraph away in the face of its explicitness.

The author undoubtedly hoped that in calling for austerity the destructive love of money would be kept at a minimum. This approach is an interesting one and raises the question as to whether, by keeping a life-style to the very minimum necessities, the person who accepts that style will lose the love of money. There seem to be a few who can. The Roman Catholic nun is a fine example. Other good examples are many of the men in the various Roman Catholic orders. In a community where there is a tight-knit sense of discipline and mutual support, men and women are able to live quite contentedly with just the bare necessities, though I can't resist recalling the Dominican priest I once knew who delighted in a very sporty and highly powered Oldsmobile, which had been given him. Driving with him was an adventure in faith, but I am sure he would never have purchased it on his own.

But, apart from a supportive community that is dedicated

to austerity along with a deep religious orientation, it is rare that the love of money disappears. Very few welfare recipients lose their love of money. Very few people will adopt austere lives voluntarily, as the minimal response to some ecologically concerned groups testifies. Very few of my friends and acquaintances have given up their automobiles for bicycles—in fact I cannot think of one, and I must include myself. It may be that the author of Timothy was writing for small, tight-knit Christian communities, in which case he may have seen this life-style as readily possible. If he was writing for a much wider audience, he may have been voicing very good advice in terms of how men may enhance their humanity, but probably he was not heeded by very many people.

The unknown author of Hebrews issues a similar warning, and makes an interesting addition when he says in Heb. 13:5, "Keep your life free from love of money, and be content with what you have; for he has said, 'I will never fail or forsake you.'" The idea that we should be content with what we have is a strong addition to the more traditional warning about the dangers of loving money. It runs counter to almost everything we believe in the context of our own culture. Part of the great American dream is to achieve more and more. People are measured by how much more they can earn. We are taught to be discontented with what we have. Contentment with our economic status is not a feeling that is prevalent in our society.

The verse also has been used as a club for those who were on the bottom of the economic pile. It is very tempting for those in positions of economic power to tell those who have no power that they should be content with what they have. Some captains of industry used this verse when dealing with the demands of the workers in the factories in the early days of the labor movement. Obviously that approach was totally unethical because the barons were unwilling, perhaps even unable, to ask themselves the same question first. Nor have matters changed much. The recent oil crisis, in which the price of crude oil increased about 400 percent and the oil refiners in this country enjoyed greatly increased profits, demonstates that neither group was content with its situation. Reasons or rationalizations were offered, but when all the economic jargon was boiled away, it all took place because those people wanted more; and once you want more, it is very easy to discover reasons why you should have it. At the same time, the rest of the world was being told to be content with its lot.

Is it possible for people to be content with what they have? I think the world would have far less aggravation if they were. The discontent over not having something cuts two ways. One way is to make people reach out and stretch themselves. Contentment means that there are no more goals to achieve, no more mountains to climb, and I am by no means sure that such a stance would be good for human beings. At the same time, discontentment with the status quo can lead to great frustration, great competition, and a devotion to economic goals, which so quickly can turn into idol worship. If it were possible to set the economic discontent into one corner, while other forms of striving after such things as insight, peace, knowledge, and personal improvement went on, we would be less likely to be slaves to the economy. Unfortunately for those who love simple solutions, mankind does not divide itself up that neatly. We will have to live with the positive and negative fruits of discontent for a much longer time and learn how to control the destructive aspects the very best we can.

The transitory nature of wealth again shows itself in the letter of James. There are several Jameses in the New Testament, and for many years this letter was attributed to the

## The Rest of the New Testament

brother of James. However, the lack of references to Jesus, or any other data that the brother of the Lord would have had, is utterly lacking, and it is probably best to classify this letter with the others that take titles from major figures, a common practice of the times.

The passage in question is James 1:9–11: "Let the lowly brother boast in his exultation, and the rich in his humiliation, because like the flower of the grass he will pass away. For the sun rises with the scorching heat and withers the grass; its flower falls, and its beauty perishes. So will the rich man fade away in the midst of his pursuits." The letter of James has a Jewish cast, and it is not surprising to see this old Jewish theme again come to the fore, though we should remember that it was also a strong theme in Stoicism, which was one visible philosophy of the time. The imagery is powerful; when the strong southwest wind blew in, a green hillside could become brown in just one day.

Of course, this theme would not be so strongly present in the Judaic–Christian tradition, and in others, if it were not so true. The parable was told by Tolstoy of the peasant to whom the devil offered all the land he could encircle in a period from sunrise to sunset. The peasant went to work with a will, but ran so hard all day that, when the sun set and he returned to the starting point, he died of exhaustion. It would seem that as long as men are going to be so persistent in pursuing that which they cannot hope to keep beyond this life, there will be those of insight in every religion who will be reminding everyone that such wealth is transitory.

We might pause here and ponder what makes man try so hard for things that can get away so easily. Some Christians and others might simply say that such people are sinners, but that kind of approach does not really get us any further. What kind of sin drives men and women in this direction? We can pierce the mystery a little farther and say that it is a sin of greed, but the question behind such a comment is, why are men greedy?

A psychologist could probably say it better, but one fact seems relatively stable. People are finite bodily creatures who, even in their finite beings, have the gift, and sometimes the curse, of being able to project beyond where they are in time and space. To the best of our knowledge, no other creature can do that in a consistent and systematic way. We are dependent for some of our satisfactions on certain tangible items, like food, the basic *things* we need. Our need for these basic tangible things on which we are dependent for life itself quickly extends itself to many other things. These are not essential in and of themselves, but because they are an extension of our imagination, they have a power over us. We want them. Some verification of this line of thinking is found in the advertising field, which so quickly makes us want things that we do not have at all and which we might never miss if we did not know they existed. Who needs an electric can opener, save maybe a handful of very weak people? But if we are told we need something often enough and skillfully enough, we begin to want it. It takes people with extra insight and motivation to push themselves away from the desire for unneeded things and toward the less tangible and more enduring aspects of life. Even in the most spiritual of places you often find imagery of wealth, such as in the description of the new Jerusalem in Revelation, which positively glows with gold and precious stones. It is hard to stay away from tangible wealth, because we are tangible creatures and so we become greedy.

Another condition of man is his difficulty in planning ahead, which tends to make that which is right now appear much more important than that which is to come. When anyone goes to buy a new car, the buyer is aware that the car has a limited life. Questions may be raised about its value three or four years hence. But that period of time is far away, and what really counts in that showroom is right now, when the paint gleams and the doors close smoothly. Sure it will get dusty, dented, and dull, but that prospect is now remote.

Some wit once said that some people can't plan more than five minutes ahead, many people can plan three months ahead, but only a handful of people can plan years or generations ahead. There is more to that comment than just an attempt at wit. I see it often in marriage counseling, where I never cease to be amazed at the number of couples who can forsee the next several months very well, but get vague much beyond that point. And to say that love is blind only partially explains it. Man is a creature who finds it hard to project himself clearly into the future, even though he possesses the ability.

If this limitation affects most people to a greater or lesser degree, it helps explain why possessions of the moment are attractive. They are projected indefinitely into the future, and it is always something of a shock when our beloved refrigerator begins to groan. "Oh, I only bought that yesterday," comes the cry, and then the realization that many yesterdays have gone by. Our instinct is that the things we have are always going to be with us, and it takes learning, a lot of learning, to understand that such is not reality. In many cases we learn much too little, much too late.

The same theme is repeated in a more violent key in James 5:1-6, where not only is the transitory nature of things again portrayed, but also the oppression the wealthy give to the poor by holding back wages, and then a hint that those who are wealthy are going to get their just deserts in the future. The vices of the wealthy we have already seen in the prophets, and this section utters the same kind of words, which point to the punishment by God for such deeds.

The underlying resentment of the less fortunate against the

## The Bible and Money

rich is felt in this section. Sometimes this resentment is overt, and people take action against the rich. Such is the stuff that makes for some revolutions. More often the resentment just lies and smoulders. The less fortunate know they probably won't get what the other person has and in some cases may even realize that they are not smart enough. Fortunes are made by a peculiar combination of brains, perseverance, and dumb luck, in varying proportions; and many of those who are resentful know that they cannot participate. That resentment is as corrosive as the acquisition of wealth itself and must be dealt with as part of the spiritual problems raised by money.

We have taken a look at many different parts of the Bible at this point and observed a variety of opinions on money. It now remains to balance the weight of the themes and draw some theological conclusions, which will give us some grasp on how Christians can most creatively deal with the opportunities and problems created by money.

### *For Further Thought*

Before we do, some questions are in order. Many groups have tried to live in a communal fashion. Some of these have been within the life of the Christian church, some have been secular. If you decided to be a part of such a group, what incentives or visions would make it possible for you to participate? The converse of that question might be more helpful to some. For what reasons did you choose not to be part of a communal life-style? Those already involved in communal living can turn these questions around. Now, having set forth your reasons, how important were the economic factors in your thinking? Your answers may give you some insight into what values you believe are important in life.

## The Rest of the New Testament

I assume that many readers are supporting some religious institution, some generously, others not so generously. Aside from specific gripes, which sometimes make you feel like spending the money on something more frivolous, what really keeps you contributing to that institution? And, considering the material we have just read on rewards for good behavior, to what extent is your giving colored by anticipation of being rewarded in some way for your support? When the first time machine is built, I would like to come back and ask the question of some medieval Christians in France or England, because I suspect the answers would be very different from the way most people would answer today.

No Christian should avoid the effort needed to honestly confront the saying from Timothy about the love of money being the root of all evils. Most readers participate comfortably in a very affluent society, fewer participate at a substandard level and would like to be more comfortable. Let that statement hit you head-on and see how you react to Timothy's proposition, and then think about your reaction. Share it in a group and see where the group reacts after wrestling with it.

# 7
# *Major Biblical Themes*

It is not difficult to handle individual Bible passages with respect to any topic. It is difficult to deal with many passages on the same topic in trying to arrive at an overall point of view. Subjectivity creeps into any theological attempt, for inevitably one's own prejudices and experiences will lead to one's emphasizing some materials while giving only cursory attention to others. Critics of the theological approach find this procedure annoying, but it does not necessarily mean that theologians are dishonest, although some are. It only means that theologians are people, dealing with the experiences of people and, what is more, dealing with the experiences of people in areas that are subtle and complex, as men and women seek to make sense out of their relationship to God.

The material with which we have been concerned in the previous chapters breaks down into four major categories. It would seem good procedure to examine each of these categories and then, in the final chapter, to set them into

*Major Biblical Themes*

some kind of perspective. The categories are not mutually exclusive, and indeed lap each other at points, but I think they have enough identity so that they may be discussed with some degree of clarity.

The first category is ==the need to control the human instincts with respect to money==. The Old Testament is far richer in this theme than the New Testament, though we can see it even there in the passages that call for an austere lifestyle. The Old Testament Hebrews were not given to much philosophical or abstract thinking; they were much more concerned with how to make life work. The incredible body of law (which confounds us in the twentieth century) that the Hebrews built up over time was designed to show people how to live together. If people followed these laws, life would be orderly and, even more, the forces that tend to tear people and communities apart would be kept under control. Life has not changed that much, either. We live under an extraordinarily large body of law, much wider than anything the Hebrews of old could have imagined. Of course, life is a lot more complex now and more law is needed.

What we overlook is the fact that our massive body of law is divorced from the religious area. I suspect very few lawyers and judges have any sense at all that in dealing with the law they are dealing with something divine. Our law is secular, completely and utterly secular, though from time to time, in certain areas of morals, religious themes creep into the conversations of lawmakers. When you come to a topic such as abortion, the rhetoric can become very religious on both sides of the issue. But when decisions on the subject are made by courts, or laws are enacted by legislatures, they are spelled out in secular terms, with secular provisions for enforcement.

Most of the Old Testament laws accept the presence of

money as a necessity of society. There is no serious attempt made to meditate abstractly on whether this money is good or bad, whether there are any alternatives to it, or whether God created it or not. It is there as a tool of society. But the law also confesses that money is a problem area for people. Passions can be aroused by it. Therefore there must be some rules and regulations with regard to its use, so that men will have some external controls working against their instinctive appetites. I doubt that the Hebrews were under any illusions that the presence of such laws would inhibit the instinctive appetites, or that the existence of a law would mean that it would be automatically obeyed.

A different approach to the same principle is seen in the New Testament in the several pastoral letters, which we can sum up as calling for an austere life-style. People should exercise enough control so that once their basic needs for food, clothing, and shelter have been met, they will not want anything further. That does not seem like very much control, but we must remember that the Old Testament laws also were considered to be in force in many early Christian communities. True, some of the cultic practices with regard to food, for instance, were not part of the early Gentile Christian churches, but it seems unlikely that the rules with regard to something like money were as quickly discarded.

One very important fact to note is that today's society has many laws that place controls on the use of money, thousands of them in fact. The concept of a minimum wage is a control on money, designed to prevent an employer from making a worker the victim of greed. People who have credit cards are informed of the limits of the interest that may be charged for overdue bills, but those notices are reminders that interest rates need to be controlled today just as surely as they needed to be controlled in the earlier Old Testament times. There is a perpetual battle between various government agencies and people who try to give false weights and measures, and even to manipulate the size and shape of boxes. People should not be defrauded when they buy their favorite breakfast cereal!

The theme of control now may be seen more easily in a very wide context. Not only is it something that is called for by the Bible, it is also something called for by every society. It is not universal in the sense that the controls placed on money are the same in every culture, but it is universal in the sense that there are monetary controls in every culture. In a world becoming increasingly interdependent it seems rather obvious that the differences in cultural controls gradually will become minimal. The recent build-up of money in the Arab world through higher oil prices highlights the way in which the need for control over money must now be considered on a world level.

Another dominant biblical theme is the fragility of money. In every section of the Old Testament, in the teaching of Jesus, and in the many New Testament letters, there are references to the transient nature of money. Jesus perhaps carried it to its ultimate extreme in Matt. 6:19–21 when he taught people not to lay up treasures on earth where they may be eroded or stolen, but to lay up treasures in heaven where nothing can take them away. But in offering us this teaching, he was drawing on the wisdom of the psalmists and prophets and inspiring later Christian writers to emphasize this point, both in the rest of the New Testament and beyond. Thousands of sermons have been preached about the fragility of wealth and the importance of paying less attention to it, because it goes so easily. The sermons will continue, because each generation is in need of learning the lesson anew. Unfortunately, most people don't live long enough, hear enough such sermons, or focus their attention enough on the more enduring things to escape the feeling that money is durable.

## The Bible and Money

We looked at some of the psychology of why people yearn for money, even when it is so fragile, in the last chapter. The question now before us is how fragile money really is. I suspect many people feel that money is one of the most tangible things in the world, and a busload of psychologists followed by a busload of bishops would not get very far in convincing most people that money is fragile. The poetic rhetoric of the Bible sounds nice from the pulpit, but it is easy to dismiss it as being the product of unworldly visionaries who don't really understand what is going on in the world.

Let us look at some of the weaknesses of money in a rather more concrete, and certainly less poetic, way. Take a dollar bill. What is it? It is a piece of paper, rather extraordinary paper at that, with a lot of printing on it. The only legal material on it of a descriptive nature is the amount, and a note telling the holder that this note is legal tender for all debts, public and private. There is a rather incongruous reminder that it is in God we trust, even when the majority of people put far more trust in that dollar bill than in God. But in the very last analysis, it is only a piece of paper, and it is worth only what someone else will exchange for it that the bearer desires.

The whole world is now observing an interesting and frightening phenomenon. The dollar bill, along with the pound, the yen, and the franc are steadily returning less and less to the bearer. The economists lecture wisely on the causes for inflation, but the knowledge we have is nowhere near adequate to solve the problem. The only way we have been able to cope with this threat in the recent decades is to throw enough people out of work so there will be less money in the hands of those who can purchase goods and services. It has something of the flavor of the old physicians who used to bleed their patients to cure them of various illnesses. If we let enough blood be shed in the system, prices may stabilize. Only this time no one is even sure whether this treatment will work because the conditions are so different. (Sometimes the patients bleed to death.)

I shouldn't be so hard on the poor economists, because I don't have the solution either, though I would suggest they consult with the psychologists much more than they do, because my financial intuition tells me that the problem has its roots in the conscious and even unconscious behavior of human beings as individuals and groups. But what is happening is that money is becoming less and less valuable. If that is not fragility of the highest order, then I don't know what is.

If a dollar bill is fragile, what about a stock certificate? Here is a piece of a company with tangible assets. The owner can drive to some point and look at a factory that is producing something, and isn't that security? But the piece of paper, which designates the owner as a part owner in the company, has a widely fluctuating value. For some time, Polaroid stock was worth quite a lot per share. In the past few months it has been worth much much less, far less than the actual drop in revenues suggests that it should be. Other stock owners are singing similar songs of woe. During the sixties many people began to feel that the value of their stocks would never go down. Now they know differently, and they, too, have a practical insight into the fragility of money. At that, we have not even looked into the fragility of companies themselves. (Once upon a time, buggy whips were a large selling item.)

We need to consider other forms of wealth to balance the view. Land, jewels, art, and precious metals seem more secure than money, as represented by dollar bills and stock certificates. Notice I have stayed away from the whole credit system, including the writing of a simple check. That is so fragile that crystal is like steel in comparison. But there is little doubt that some of these tangible assets have more enduring value. Diamonds have been a girl's best friend for a long time, because there have been very few periods in history when diamonds were not valuable. But jewels, precious metals, and art can all be stolen. Art is a very fluctuating thing, and the taste of the day can play havoc with the value of a picture. If you pay $500 for a picture, and six years later the art world decides that it is only worth $300 because the picture is passé, you will think the value of your art is very fragile. Land probably has had the most enduring value over the centuries of civilization, but even here it is a cumbersome form of wealth. It is awkward to translate eighty acres into food, cars, and toothpaste.

The evidence is overwhelming that money is fragile. The so-called unworldly visionaries have had a far more comprehensive view of what money is. No Christian and no non-Christian can ever have a complete theology of money unless he or she can come to terms with the truth that money is extremely fragile. That does not necessarily mean that anyone should totally dismiss money, but that he should understand its evanescent nature.

There is a significant amount of material in the Bible about the corrupting nature of money. Perhaps the strongest statement is the one from Timothy on the love of money being the root of all evils, but it has its rivals in such places as Isaiah, who tried to show the horrible effect it had upon people. Jesus saw it as a prime barrier to the Kingdom of God. The reader can check back on the other writings, but when they are all added together, they represent a forceful set of teachings about the evils inherent in the pursuit, holding, and spending of money. Roman Catholic holy orders often take these teachings very seriously and demand a vow of poverty in order to keep the corrupting force of money at bay.

It should not be necessary to review the overwhelming evidence that money corrupts. Father and son have turned against one another, people with money have treated people

*Major Biblical Themes*

without it disgracefully, and greed has always been one of the ugliest passions. An incredible amount of crime is connected with it. It has always been true, and no major society has been free of these problems. No major religion has ever endorsed money as a benificent force, and most of them have been acutely aware of the corrupting force it has.

But why is this fact so painfully true? A full analysis deserves the attention of concerned psychologists, but there is some observable data, which could provide a partial answer. First of all, money means survival, probably more so in our industrial society than in some of the agrarian societies of the past. If a person has no money and cannot rely on sources that have some, that person is in grave danger. There will be no food, no shelter, no health care, there will be none of the things that keep people alive. Now it may seem ridiculous in an affluent land, with a welfare system that keeps many people alive, to suggest such a thing. But that welfare system is an alternate source of money for most people. Suppose it did not exist. Some would find other individuals who had money and survive. But those who could not, and who could not or would not steal, would starve and be homeless.

We have only to take a look at the people in the famine-ravaged areas of the world. Even in India and the sub-Sahara, those people who have more than an average amount of money are eating, not well in many cases, but food flows where the money is. Those below a certain point just do not receive the money and therefore don't have the food. Now I know that there is a limit beyond which food will not stretch and that world hunger is more complex than just the lack of money. True, a person with no money could grow enough food to survive, but in the cooler climates, without shelter and an ability to preserve the food through the periods when no food could be grown, food would be meager.

For almost anyone reading this book this line of thought

*101*

may seem rather radical, but I suggest strongly that you test it. There is enough money in this country to keep people alive, though the distribution system often assures some that keeping alive is just about all they can expect. But the essence of the human situation is that money means survival.

That need for survival provides an incentive to get the money. It may not seem that such incentives exist for those on welfare. But it is often a question of what the system offers. If you took welfare away, most people would not lie down and die. A few would go to work, and those unable to get work would steal. I suppose there would be some, particularly among the elderly, who would literally just lie down and die. Those who are so hypercritical of the welfare system need to ask themselves what would happen if there were no such thing, and millions of people suddenly were cut off from that means of support. More particularly, they should ask themselves whether they would be willing to endure the higher crime rate that would inevitably ensue. The need to survive somehow is very strong in most human beings.

A second reason money is corrupting is that money is a source of power, and philosophers, from Lord Acton on down, have voiced the view that power is corrupting. A good example of that philosophy in action was in the recent Congressional examination of Nelson Rockefeller. Over and over again the congressmen demonstrated their concern over the immense power that Rockefeller could wield in the office of vice-president because of his vast wealth. In his turn, Rockefeller played down his power, sometimes almost appearing naive about his wealth. It was interesting that almost no congressmen could identify a specific act as clearly demonstrating control over any significant part of the economy, and no one did in any major way. Still, they felt that he would instinctively lean toward the forces of big business at the expense of those with less power and money.

*Major Biblical Themes*

Moving from such extreme examples to the rest of the people, it does not seem possible to deny that money does mean power. Now that power is not always bad. If you have a leaky pipe, your money is the power that will bring the plumber to your rescue. You may take that power for granted, but try getting that plumber to come without the money and see what happens. In the normal course of events this kind of power is natural, and we all do take it for granted. But, using our plumber again, suppose you want him to come right away, and he tells you he has three jobs ahead of yours. You have some extra money, and so you tell him that there is an extra $20 if he will put aside the other jobs and come right over. Now your money has begun to corrupt you, and if the plumber accepts the bribe, money has had a corrupting influence on him.

The world is full of instances where people have used money to accomplish their ends at the expense of other people, in one way or another, even to the ultimate example of purchasing a murder. Every day our newspapers are full of such stories. The biblical writers could see this problem just as clearly as we can and responded to this corrupting power with severe warnings about money.

We need to identify a problem on the other side of the coin, which is less obvious but equally as important. ==The absence of power in human life is corrupting.== When a person feels that he or she can do nothing to positively affect the course of life, that person becomes frustrated and either retreats into a shell or strikes out angrily at the world. Now this sense of powerlessness is not limited simply to money. The police once arrested a youth from a wealthy family for tipping over gravestones. When asked why he did it, he replied that it was the only way he could make his parents pay some attention to him. But much vandalism is carried out by people who are powerless because they don't have any money for things they would like to do, and so they express their powerlessness through destructiveness, as a kind of retribution.

It is easy to point a finger at such people and tell them they should exhibit more control. Of course they should, and society needs to be protected from those who cannot exercise this control. At the same time, those who would not think of behaving badly should appreciate the enormous frustration that can build up inside another human being when he feels powerless, particularly with respect to money. Television has been a special irritant here, because virtually everyone has his nose rubbed in the things that money can buy, and those who cannot buy feel desperately left out of what the majority are doing. So it is necessary to acknowledge that a lack of money beyond a certain point is corrupting, both to the individual and to society as well, as that person vents his frustration and bitterness on those around him.

The last major strain in the Bible is the creative and positive aspect of money. Whether we are dealing with Solomon's view of money as a reward for virtue, or with those writers who saw there was a need for money, both to support the religious institution and as a way of extending generosity, we must not ignore these positive passages. As a pastor I am constantly being impressed with the necessity of having enough money to manage the local instituion, and it has always been that way from the time of the Old Testament law to the present. Whatever else the church has had to say about money, it always has persuaded people to part with a portion of their money to keep the religious institution going. It doesn't matter whether we are talking about a parish with 5,000 members or 50, all of them have budgets tailored to fit local circumstances.

Some idealists look upon this situation as an evil. Attempts have been made over the ages to form little cells of people who would be able to worship together, study together, and act in the name of Christ together without being involved in professional ministries, and special buildings, which are the two main items that require money in the life of the church. There is a lot to be said for this kind of church, but one fact stands out historically. It is viable only for a minute fraction of those who would be followers of Christ. For the vast majority of Christians, the life of the church centers around professional ministries and special buildings, which cost money.

In this context it becomes hard to avoid the fact that money is a means by which the religious life of people is carried on in an organized fashion. Despite what we can do as individuals, we must eventually come together as the Body of Christ to fully participate in the religious life, combining our strengths and ministering to our weaknesses. And perhaps it is time to stop browbeating ourselves and start from the premise that money can be one way that Christians can express their faith. The Christian faith has long proclaimed that people must give of themselves in response to what God has given them, and there are three basic things in human life that people can give: time, talent, and money. Taken together, they are what is basically meant by giving one's self to God. I suppose someone will be unkind enough to recall that Jesus never gave any money to the religious enterprise that we know about and to remind us that he taught that those who had received so freely must give freely of their talents. A minister who fails to keep this teaching in mind runs some great risks.

But Jesus was not concerned about the organization and maintenance of a religious institution. He made no effort to organize his followers into groups of any kind to carry on his work. The reference in Matthew to the church is the only one of its kind in the Gospels, and all other material points away from an organized approach in the mind of Jesus. However, to say that because Jesus did not organize it, therefore it is a necessary evil, and that its financial support is a necessary evil is far too radical a conclusion. Jesus was critical of the weaknesses and corruption in the religious institution of his day, and he would be critical of the weaknesses and corruption in our institutions as well. If we may feel free to acknowledge that the end of history did not take place exactly as Jesus taught, then we should feel free to accept the church as that institution in which people gather to seek the Lord of life, and that institution does not automatically divest itself of all qualities inherent in human organizations. In the case of the church, that fact means professional leadership and special buildings. That fact in turn means that money must be raised, as it has from the days of Paul onward, and this process can be helpful in building a Christian sense of stewardship and generosity.

There are a lot of problems with the use of this money. Take the special buildings erected to the glory of God. One of my favorite religious places is the Cathedral of St. John the Divine in New York. It is not yet finished, and millions of dollars already have gone into its construction. It is absolutely magnificent, and when I wander in I am carried to a kind of ecstasy as I see visually what is meant by the magnificence of God. Down the hill lies Harlem in all its human misery. Granted that all the money in the cathedral would not have solved all the problems in Harlem, it would still have gone a long, long way in the relief of human misery. Critics of the cathedral have flogged its builders with that sentiment for several decades now, pointing out that people become too attached to their religious buildings and sink much too much money into them. I have often concurred in such sentiments, having watched what all pastors watch as people idolize the building and forego the human ministries to the people that Christ called us all to carry out.

But would any ministries become reality without the building? Some would, there are always a few people for whom the sanctuary is low in priority. However, human experience seems to tell us that, for most people, the building is a necessity before human ministries become incarnate. It is unfortunate that such is the human situation, and the best the professionals can do is to work constantly to keep the use of the money in some kind of realistic proportion between the building and the ministry. There is no magic formula for this division, though I sometimes wish there were; all we can do is to be keenly aware that the building must not become an idol and that the human situation must receive its share. That is a difficult fight, because the building is tangible and it also stands for a lot of things in its tangibility. Ministries to the poor, the victimized, the powerless, and the hopeless will always have to fight the uphill battle for the religious dollar, while the debate goes on endlessly about how money can serve God most effectively.

For those who despair, I can only say that if people were generous and loving with their money, as the church tries to teach them to be, there would be little need for the church, at least in the form it now has. It is the will of Christ that we be generous, and the church is one place where that teaching is carried out, sometimes well, sometimes poorly, but it goes on. It is always a call for Christian rejoicing when an individual learns to give generously and warmly, because a whole host of other Christian virtues can and do accompany such learning.

What of Solomon's teaching that money is the result of virtue? The usual response to this kind of teaching is the stereotype of the Puritan, who was sober, industrious, and successful. Sermons abounded in those days with the lambasting of the poor for their lack of virtue, so clearly demonstrated to the wealthy by the fact of poverty. it seems to me

*The Bible and Money*

that here is another case of life not being as simple as we would like it to be.

First of all, money can be acquired by virtuous work. We have already discussed many of the situations where money is acquired by nonvirtuous effort, but we cannot let those blind us to the fact that, for most people, money is obtained through steady work. The amount received varies and does not always make sense. There is a lot of wailing done about the fact that people don't want to work any more, as if they ever did, but, in point of fact, most males and an increasingly large number of females derive a large part of their satisfaction and identity from their work. Boring work in particular never has been very popular, whether it was done by the medieval peasant plowing furrows or by the modern assembly-line worker tightening nuts; but people do it, both to survive and to feel a sense of being. Although the evidence is scattered and inconclusive, there seems to be some trend toward more meaningful kinds of work, rather than away from work, which I would suggest comes from the ever-increasing education people are receiving in our society, which has the effect of raising horizons and expectations, even about work. But in all cases it pays off in money.

Second, we must be more cautious about disparaging the poor for a lack of virtue. People are poor for a wide variety of reasons. Some are poor because they are not very intelligent, some because they have no foresight, some because they lack the incentive to fight in the economic system, some simply because they have run into bad breaks over which they had little or no control. I just cannot agree with the ancient and modern puritans that poverty equals vice. If I had been born with an IQ of 72, I would probably be poor, and would resent someone saying I was poor because I was bad.

Third, Solomon exaggerated the virtue of great wealth. If

we have any religious streak at all, we often seek to justify our actions—and sometimes even if we are not particularly religious. Solomon enjoyed his riches. Furthermore, he worked for them. He was a smart king, a foresighted king, and he had the gift of earning great money. What he overlooked in the human situation is the fact that great wealth is not proportionate to the effort or intelligence involved in earning money. The comparisons are risky, because no one has yet worked out an objective scale, and probably never will. To take an example from close to home, the intelligence, effort, complexity of job, and responsibility that goes into being a good minister is certainly equal in many respects to what it takes to run a good-sized company. The good minister in our current structure will make the cash equivalent of around $20,000, and the company president may make $75,000. Once you get beyond a certain point in talent, the external circumstances begin to have a lot more to do with what you earn. It would seem that the chief executives of those companies, which pay them well up in the six-figure bracket are not often two to five times as talented as their peers in smaller or less lucrative situations.

Thus while it would seem perfectly legitimate to say that money is a proper reward for virtue and industry, there is a decided risk in pushing too far in an attempt to justify great wealth. Not that I have anything in particular against great wealth, but I am going to be most wary in attributing virtue and even skill to people in direct proportion to their wealth.

These themes of control, frugility, corruption, and virtue seem to be the basic ones in the Bible. There are various smaller categories that can fit in under these, but basically these four give us the frame of reference in which people may determine what a consistent Christian theology might be. I will attempt to outline this in the following chapter.

### For Further Thought

I think it is hard to argue with the biblical evidence as to what the major themes are, but there is a serious question of the weight they bear with respect to one another. The themes of control and fragility can be given positive emphasis or negative emphasis. Corruption is clearly a negative aspect, and its virtues of course are positive. I think the reader needs to weigh these topics carefully in light of the writings we have examined and to test where the balance ultimately comes. The trick is to do this honestly and not simply embrace the passages with which one instinctively agrees and dismiss all those of a contrary nature. Does one theme ultimately dominate your feeling, or do you sense that here are four basic strands, which need to be kept in some kind of tension?

# 8
# *A Theology of Money*

Almost anyone can dig up facts if they are patient enough. I marvel at people who have counted the number of *ands* in the Bible. The harder task is to set the evidence before us and decide what conclusions may be drawn from it. Here reasonable people may differ—and differ all the more in matters of faith. For the fact remains that one person will give more weight to some factors than another person will, and the underlying reasons for this are often hard to perceive. The reasons come out of our backgrounds, our experiences, and sometimes even our dreams. So I trust that my readers will take my thoughts seriously but feel free to work out improvements where they may be helpful.

I do not think it is possible to give a simple answer to the question about what God wants us to believe about money. Sometimes there are simple answers to hard questions, but I just cannot believe that this is one of those times. Take just one simple idea that people occasionally voice: Follow the teachings of Jesus and give everything you have away. There are a few people who have actually done such a charitable act and caused great joy in the lives of others. But if we were to make that act the only way to deal with money, what kind of a world would it be? Utterly chaotic is the answer. It would not be long before the means of creating wealth would become disoriented, and more people would suffer than ever before. The same truth follows almost any simplistic argument; pushed to its logical conclusion, it would result in serious problems.

Let us start in quite a different fashion and make a few basic assumptions. Not that these assumptions are cast in concrete. They can be argued, but it is impossible to draw any kind of conclusions in any kind of study without admitting to some prior assumptions. The sin is to conceal them, and unfortunately religious thinkers are often masters in disguising their assumptions. I will try not to do that, though I am well aware that some critic will point out that I may not be infallible.

My first assumption is that the world is going to carry on for awhile. The Christian must be prepared to live in an ongoing community. Such an assumption does not void the several teachings of Jesus about the coming of the Kingdom suddenly and without warning and the subsequent necessity of being ready. But to ignore the ongoing world is to ultimately sanction the victories of evil, and no Christian can afford to do that. I grant that my assumption is a little rash. We may be impulsive enough to incinerate ourselves with the atomic bomb or pigheaded enough to poison ourselves with the waste we produce; we cannot ignore those possibilities. However, one of the most effective ways to avoid these catastrophies is to treat the world as an ongoing, long-range proposition, and I think it is a good approach for both Christian and non-Christian to take.

## A Theology of Money

There will be things in that ongoing society that may not be healthy or just. The Christian will always need the prophetic word to call that society to account and to be one of the factors that will help to keep it from self-destruction. There is no guarantee that destruction may not come, but the Christian has never really sought guarantees about anything in this world.

If the society is to endure, the second assumption we should make is that money will be a part of it. It is totally beyond my comprehension how any society beyond the most primitive could function without some acceptable medium of exchange with which a person could buy or sell services and goods—which again is what money is. When we observe the corruption that too often attends money, we are tempted to create a society in which money is not necessary. But I believe that if we could do away with money tomorrow, we would have to take it up again the day after tomorrow. If I seem to be laboring the obvious, it is only because I know that some segments of the Christian community see money only as evil; and though they cannot do without it, they would like to exorcise it from their midst, which puts them in a very difficult and, I think, uncreative position. To treat money as though it ought to be flushed into the sewer, while not being able to do without it, has the same kind of effect as taking drugs. I suppose it is possible for very small groups to withdraw totally from the commercial aspects of society, but I cannot see such a movement as having widespread impact—nor should it have.

If the world is going to go on, and money is going to be a part of that world, then my third assumption is that the Christian must learn to live with money. That sounds simple, but, in point of fact, even economists who deal with money all the time have difficulty living with it. Money has sort of a

## The Bible and Money

mystic haze around it, and it is often treated by economists much as the ancient high priests treated the holy of holies. If you doubt it, read John K. Galbraith's *Money: Where It Came, Whence It Went*, Houghton-Mifflin, 1975) and you will quickly see how money has baffled intelligent people for a long time. People develop attitudes and expectations about the way money works, which become utterly crystallized, as rigid and as brittle as an icicle; and the history of money is a history of people discovering that money steadily changes the way it works. We were not supposed to be able to have inflation and recession at the same time, according to the truly brilliant Lord Keynes, but Keynes failed to appreciate the change wrought by corporations and unions so large and powerful that they were able to overcome the previous bounds of supply and demand.

Therefore, it is no easy task for a Christian to learn to live with money on an ongoing basis. Our guidelines are far more subtle and important than the technical aspects of economic theory. But I think we can gain some degree of understanding if we look at our four basic themes and express them in terms of a polarity: Money is both intensely useful and intensely dangerous. The Bible writers repeatedly point out the dangers of money, its ability to corrupt, to arouse dark and selfish passions in people. It points out the creative aspects in seeing it as the fruit of proper labor. It is the reward theme that keeps the biblical doctrine of money from being completely negative, and so I believe it essential that a Christian view of money be one of polarity.

That polarity is intense. Money is like atomic power—or the girl with the curl—when it is good, it is very, very good, but when it is bad, it is horrid. How else can we account for some of the extreme biblical statements, such as the love of money being the root of all evils? The Bible writers were well aware of the dynamic power of money. They were not then in

## A Theology of Money

a position to see the measure of comfort and safety that money has brought through its funding of our technological society; but, in simple terms, such as in the story of Solomon and the pronouncement of rewards by the last Isaiah, they testified that money could be a good thing. Add that to the consistent provision for the financial support of the religious institution, and I see it as difficult to avoid the conclusion that money has an intense and active polarity in the life of society. If we look at money in this way, I think we grasp the essence of biblical thinking.

To help us learn to think this way, let us take a further look at some of the destructive aspects of money. And I want to stress that it will be helpful if we can keep the distinction between destructive and evil in our minds. Evil implies that the money in and of itself has a dark quality, like a poison. It doesn't. Destructive implies that it can do damage if uncontrolled, like fire or atomic power, but allows the positive options to be considered.

Money is destructive and dangerous because it arouses dark passions in people. The biblical evidence is extensive, and the experiences of most people back up the evidence. Money can make people greedy, indifferent, indolent, violent, and selfish. People grow to love it for what it will buy, and in some cases they will grow to love it just for itself, as did King Midas in the old legend. The love of money may not be the root of all evils, but it is the root of a substantial amount of evil.

It is unlikely that the government will ever print a warning on all its currency that money is a health hazard, but they could. And just to complicate matters, money represents different levels of danger to different people. It is much like alcohol. There are some people who cannot touch a drop of alcohol without an irresistible craving for more coming over them. There are many others who can drink and avoid the serious consequences. The important difference between money and alcohol is that the alcoholic can give up his booze and thus avoid injury, while we all are virtually locked into the use of money. As a practical matter, disregarding a minority of the population, all of us must utilize money every day of our lives, and for some people this utilization is a very real problem.

What can we do about this problem? There have been many responses to this difficulty. Some people have been told to give up money, but that is not a very realistic solution for most of us. Smokers can take up chewing gum as an alternative, and there are substitutes for various other dangerous habits, but there are no substitutes for money. A very common response is to just ignore the danger, with the usual disastrous results that come from willfully ignoring any danger. Life has enough unknown dangers without courting trouble from known sources. A precious few can skate on thin ice without falling through, but most of us wind up getting wet. To try to breeze through life hoping that money will not be a problem is to invite the severe sins that money can bring about.

The best response is to become thoroughly aware of all the dangers that money poses, to understand how it can lead us in some of the negative directions that the Bible describes so well. Now I realize that knowledge is not an invincible barrier to sin, despite what Plato suggested. Paul had a better insight into human nature when he observed that the things he knew perfectly well were bad he went ahead and did anyway. There are always people who will know perfectly well what is good and what is bad, and wind up choosing the bad. However, such insight should never lead Christians into thinking that the opposite must be right, that knowledge has nothing to do with good and bad behavior. Knowledge can be a help in avoiding danger. If I see a sign telling me about some thin ice, I am much less apt to get wet than if there is no sign at all. If we understand the various ways in which money has corrupted people in the past, we will be less apt to stumble into the same traps.

Flowing directly out of this knowledge is an increased awareness of the need for appropriate controls. We have controls on all kinds of dangerous things in society. We need fire permits from the fire department, and drivers' licenses to drive our cars. They are controls designed to reduce danger and increase effectiveness. A principal part of any body of Christian thought about money must accept the Old Testament witness that money must be controlled. The Hebrews had rules, rules that helped to minimize the dangerous side of money. If you could not legally charge your brother interest, you were less likely to take advantage of him.

The problem comes in thinking that the rules that were adequate in biblical times will also be adequate for our times. Some of them would be, for there are still many small personal transactions that we all make. But there is a world of difference between the biblical economic world and our world, with its credit system, multinational corporations, advertising, and technological skills. We must learn some new rules, based on the spirit of the old ones, to help us control the dynamic economic forces around us. That is hard, for we tend to fall behind in our perception of where economics really is at any moment.

Some might argue that human nature does not change, and therefore the old rules will be adequate. I agree that the same power drives, the same greed, the same pride, the same grabbing after fast and easy money are still very much a part of the scene. There is nothing basically new in human sin. But the framework of the sins changes, in some areas more than in others. The framework of sexual sins is largely unchanged; unfaithfulness, exploitation, anger, and lust are all present.

The major changes have been the curing of disease and the qualitative improvements in contraception. Those people who think they are out on the fringe of something new and daring are bad historians. Men and women have harmed each other sexually by depersonalization, selfishness, and manipulation all along. Likewise, the great joys are still with us, enhanced by the lessening of fear through our better medical knowledge.

The framework of economic sins has changed a lot. There are many many more economic institutions with far more interrelationships than ever before. The same dark forces that have corrupted people in the past now have many new avenues to use, and we need to think about controls in these areas. We need to find out how we can be just and merciful in a much more complicated situation.

Some of the controls are extensions of those found in the Bible. The limitation of interest rates is a prime example. The ancient Hebrews, the medieval moneylenders, and our modern bankers all have had a concern about the control of interest rates. In biblical times it was a fairly simple matter. Today it is a very complex one. There is a terrific tension between the need to keep interest rates up so money will be put to work and the need to keep them low enough so that a sufficient number of people can afford to avail themselves of credit. We are in a curious bind at the moment, as we watch the government borrow vast sums of money and offer higher interest rates than the banks so that there is relatively little money for housing and it is offered at higher rates than has been common for the last few decades.

But it is incredible to try to contemplate what could happen if anyone intervened in the system. If the banks are allowed to charge interest rates as high as those offered by government bonds, the government cannot finance its legislation. Some people will shout with glee. If anyone tries to legislate lower interest rates for mortgages, then no money will flow in as long as other interest rates are high. It is a fine example of the old principle that you can never do just one thing. There is no question that controls are needed, but there are a lot of questions about which controls will allow the best and fairest balance. One thing is sure, no one can have interest rates that meet only their needs, a compromise is needed, and it is a very hard one to strike in the face of the many self-interested parties involved.

An example of control that was not needed in ancient Israel is a control on economic concentration, known in our day as a monopoly. The extremes of the problem are well known. When economic power becomes so concentrated as to permit a company to charge whatever it pleases, regardless of cost or profit, then it is unjust. Theoretically our economic system is based on the premise that there is such an animal as free enterprise, where enough competition exists between companies to exert a limiting factor on their power.

In point of fact, the free enterprise system does not exist in many parts of our economy. The utilities are the best known example. Each electric company is given an area in which to work and in which it enjoys freedom to sell electricity without competition. In return for this freedom, the company must limit its rate of return to a certain percentage of its economic value. How that value is determined is a subject of intense debate every time a rate case comes up. The company finds ways to expand the base, the state argues that the base should be severely limited. Out of the debate comes some measure of justice, with both company and consumer absolutely sure that they are getting robbed blind, as they sometimes are.

Other commercial areas are only slightly less restrictive. There are very few automobile companies, very few major food processors, very few airplane manufacturers, and very few of many other kinds of companies. Power becomes concentrated enough so that these few companies in each area have the power to control prices as they please, and entry into their field is very limited. How long has it been since a major new car manufacturer entered the arena against the big three? We have seen a clear example of that power in recent years, when companies have kept on increasing prices in the face of falling demand, an unthinkable situation in classic free-enterprise economics.

Out of this concentration comes abuse. Several years ago some electric equipment manufacturers were found guilty of price-fixing. The oil companies move their prices in lockstep. The airlines amuse us with their variations on the theme that "no one charges lower prices," since they have taken great care to see that the controlling bodies do not let them. Nor should we be surprised. Part of human nature is to acquire, to get the most, and companies behave like individuals in this regard. It is so tempting to want to cut the corner a little finer, to earn just a little more. The motive is no different than the grain merchant of Israel who wanted to earn a little more and so cheated on the size of his measure. The result today, when power is so concentrated, is much more overwhelming.

So we need controls. I do not want to get into all the ways in which these controls might be implemented, without making the economy less productive; that is a book by itself. What our biblical understanding tells us is that in these new areas of huge monopoly, controls are needed. And not only are they needed, but needed in such a way that those who control do not wind up being alter egos for the companies. That is not so easy, even a busload of bishops might be tempted to protect instead of to control.

Another area where controls are needed is an old one with many new twists. That is the area of those who are at the very

## A Theology of Money

bottom of the money pile. The Bible clearly teaches that the care of the poor is a moral responsibility, so that the themes of caring and control now intersect. We need one set of controls to provide the money for the poor, and that is done currently via the tax system. Without the tax system there seems little doubt that most of the poor would starve. There would always be some charity, for many humans are compassionate, but can you imagine how well the welfare system would work if each person earning money could or could not contribute voluntarily? Then there must be controls on the use of the money, for there are always those who want to receive more than any system will allow. The poor are no more virtuous than the rich, and usually are much more desperate. We are struggling with these problems at all levels of government and are trying to work out ways that are just and that at the same time can be afforded.

It is difficult to be rational in this area of money. My ministry has taken me into some welfare homes, and I recall very well a sense of outrage in seeing a large color TV set in one of them. The critics of the system love to exploit such stories. But just as you decide that all people are crooks, you walk into a home where people are undernourished or cold. They don't have the brains to beat the system, and they must watch helplessly while a little TV set shows them a hundred scenes a day about how well most people live. Money lets these people live, without it they would starve, and any Christian thought must be involved with the controls necessary to provide it, as well as the controls necessary to keep the recipients under control. There is danger on two fronts, not on one.

With such a thought, we can move to a further consideration of the positive side of money. The Christian needs to understand the positive side of money, too. It is one of the things that allows us to live in society. There are various

## The Bible and Money

points of view about whether primitive man had money and, if he did, how it functioned. Property was much more a shared thing. But in anything but the most primitive cultures there was something used as money: shells, teeth, or stones. As societies evolved, money became the key ingredient in giving people the necessities of life, food, clothing, shelter, and, we might well want to add, medical care. It is not surprising that anything that essential gathered a religious kind of quality, such as its essentiality, its life-giving aspects, its mystery, its ability to bring other kinds of rewards (property and goods). Of course it can become an idol and often has. It still is. But it lets us live in a complex society.

What is even more important is that money is one ingredient in relieving some kinds of suffering. A person is hungry and needs food. Somewhere in our society the money must be found to provide it. The problem is seen at its greatest in the dreadful spectacle of world hunger, with half a billion people suffering from malnutrition. Christian groups are working hard to collect money to help relieve some of the worst of this hunger. It is only a small amount, but the relief of suffering it brings is enormous for its recipients.

The same kind relief exists in medical aid. Some years ago I was in a hospital in Vadalla, India, on a United Church of Christ tour and saw a woman writhing in agony on the floor. Our guide explained she had bugs in her nose, and the doctor would have to remove them. Some of our mission money was being used to finance that hospital and that doctor, and that woman was going to get relief. That kind of medical problem is not a rarity here, just in a different key. There are many medical conditions that can only be cured by fantastically expensive techniques and equipment, and money often means the difference between getting relief and suffering.

At other positive aspect of money is its support of organized religion. I can just feel the arrows heading my way from all the people who see organized religion as a fraud of some kind or other. But I am not so pessimistic. Money performs an overall good in supporting organized religion. The religious venture of Christians, which is what I know better than any others, is rarely carried out alone. Only truly extraordinary individuals can do it. Even then, the church as we know it is always in the background. For most religious people it is in the foreground, comprising a gathered fellowship of faith in which people mutually support each other. There are all kinds of failings in this organized religious enterprise, and many of the severe criticisms are often accurate. Where the criticisms fall short is that, even after all is said and done, the church persists because people need it.

To operate, the church needs money. There are a few religious bodies that operate without paid professionals, but not many. It may not need a special building in the strictest sense of the word need, but it usually winds up with one. Music is one means by which something of the beauty of the divine is conveyed and through which prayer and praise is offered to God, and that music is not free. Programs of education, social action, and compassion are carried out in the name and spirit of Christ, and they need money. The giving of the money is not selfless in some respects because most individuals expect something in return, and yet even those expectations do not explain the whole phenomenon. The organization needs support to operate, but there is something beyond that.

The money is also a way to extend oneself on behalf of others. The giving of money opens us up as people. It expands our sensitivities. It enables us to be creative, and I feel that one of the ways in which we are most significantly made in the image of God is in our creativity. When we are able to use our money in creative, unselfish ways, money becomes a positive good in our lives, as well as helping the people who receive it directly or benefit by its products. Thus the church encourages us at a point where we can be expanded greatly as people.

However, the anticlerical streak in many people may lead them to feel that the professional clergy encourage this giving to feather their own nests. Honesty requires the admission that there always have been some religious frauds around, who have milked well-meaning people for all they could get in the name of the divine. They encouraged generosity in others, but not in themselves. However, most Protestant clergy are not paid very well, and have to struggle to get any raises at all, let alone enjoy a salary that most people with comparable training and responsibility would consider as demeaning. Catholic clergy enjoy much comfort from their compensation, but seldom wind up leaving a large estate to anyone. On balance, the clergy of our society work hard for relatively little, and so the accusation of milking people unfairly just will not stand up, except in isolated cases.

Therefore, the support of the church is a good and proper use for money. When everyone becomes a classic saint, we just might be able to do without as much, but that day is a long way off. Until then, good is accomplished through money by allowing the church to function, not always efficiently, not always effectively, but ever seeking ways to help people draw closer to God, to achieve some meaning for their lives, and opening concrete opportunities to help other people in a variety of ways.

It is very tempting to look at money and how it is used and misused, and begin to think that if we only could change the system, then the evils of money would be reduced and the positive side would flourish. So we tinker with the system we have or propose to change the system more radically.

The major challenge to the free enterprise system we have is that of socialism, and we need to take a moment to consider whether the evil side effects of money would be reduced under socialist leadership. It is a tempting proposition. If we could just get the production out of the hands of those greedy capitalists and let the people run it, the workers, the ordinary people. It sounds good. The capitalist system runs on the premise that the individual desires to maximize his return on investment; that if risks are taken those who assume the risks should be rewarded proportionately higher than those who take no risks but simply labor for the corporation. At first glance it looks as though the greed that fuels much of the capitalist system could be eliminated under government and/or worker ownership of the major parts of production.

But if we consider the teachings of the Bible about how people behave with respect to money, socialism does not seem to be the cure to the polarity of money. The first weakness in the socialist system is that sainthood, wisdom, and restraint are not conferred in greater measure upon governments or employees than on owners. No thinking Christian can accept a premise that some classes or groups are more saintly than others. Sin is a human phenomenon from which no one is exempt. Socialist countries seem to have a large measure of economic sin too. People get ripped off, an elitist class comes to the front, and productivity is not noticeably better. In fact, it is usually worse.

A second source of evil in the socialist system, where the government owns and operates the major areas of production, is the concentration of power. When political power and economic power are in the hands of the same people, the potential for corruption is greatly increased. Power corrupts, and one of the reasons that this country has had such long-term high morality in many areas is because there has been not only a separation of powers in the three basic areas of government but also a separation of economic and political power.

There are places in our society where there is very close

*The Bible and Money*

alliance between government and industry. We do not live in what college textbooks like to think of as classic free enterprise. The FAA and the airlines play a very close game, the ICC and the truckers do likewise, and some corruption has appeared around the interfaces of these groups. To further ally government and industry, even in our democratic society, is to run the very high risk that accompanies concentration of power, and it neither would seem to be good common sense nor good Christian ethics to encourage such alliances.

I am not exonerating capitalism in this analysis. It has been a very productive system for us and has brought us a high standard of living, from which even its fiercest critics derive comfort. But it has been very wasteful, it has been manipulative, it has been criminal at some points. It is often simply unmanageable. Right now we have a very high unemployment rate, varying as these pages are written; but we seem to be in a period where 7 to 9 percent of the workers can't find any work. The system does not correct itself easily, and in the meantime a lot of people suffer. The experience of rising to a given standard of living and then having it yanked away is a very disrupting one. Identity crises are common in people who lose jobs. Houses are lost, kids are brought home from college, diets are altered. We really do not know how to make the capitalist system work as fairly as Christian love would have it do.

Therefore, it is not the system that reduces evil and promotes good. I feel that the search for a system that will bypass human sin is a futile one, and energy can be more profitably spent in asking about controls, the best trade-off between concentration and economy of scale, and the care of those who cannot compete in the system.

Another solution to the polarity of money often voiced, is to return to a simple life, with less money and less goods. Then people would not be so greedy and we would not be so

## A Theology of Money

wasteful. The people who argue that way see the economic system as a big engine. All we need to do is slow it down. Then we would live better, enjoy life more, and the good uses of money would be enhanced.

The problem with that approach to the simple life, which has a distinctly Christian tone to it, is that the model in mind is the wrong one. Our economy is not one big engine; it is a multitude of interrelated smaller ones, all going at once, like a Rube Goldberg machine. If you intervene anywhere, the results are often not what you want.

Take the cars. They complicate our life. They cost a lot of money, they use a lot of natural resources, and they pollute the air. They also kill 50,000 people a year. Certainly a lower standard of living would involve greatly restricted use of the automobile. The energy crisis is already making us think seriously about this.

But the complexities of that restriction are enormous. The economic impact on all the people put out of automobile-related jobs would be enormous. Even assuming some cars were made, millions of people would be out of work. The housing patterns of our society are based on transportation by car. How long would it take to organize public transportation, so that all the people who work in firms along the thirty miles of Rte. 128 outside of Boston, for instance, could get to work in a reasonable time? The problems are staggering. They may well be soluble, most certainly in a technical sense, but the reorienting of people's patterns requires motivation, incentive, and time.

Eventually the simpler life will be forced on us to some degree. We have lived as well as most of us are going to live. Some will do better, but not many. To allocate money in an age of scarcity, to distribute goods and services fairly is going to ask a lot of people; and so far we have shown little ability to plan how it is all going to take place. Human beings are remarkably adaptive and clever creatures, and I have some hope that we will learn how to live with less. But I think the pain of adjustment will be very great. A lot of the freedom we now take for granted will be lost or restricted, such as the freedom to travel where we want, exactly when we want to go.

But this simpler life will not change the basic problem of money. It is still going to be a tool of society. It is still going to have its potential for evil and for good. It is going to tempt people into illegal and immoral means of getting it and keeping it. And with less and less to spread around to more and more people, in terms of buying power, the strains of how it is earned and distributed will be greater and greater as time goes on. It will continue to be fragile. It will lead people into corruption. It will need more and more sophisticated controls. All these factors will call upon us to develop the best solutions in the light of human need, human aspirations, and human dignity that we can find at a given moment. Our best brains will be needed to solve such problems, not only technically, but psychologically and morally, as well. The biblical principles we have seen will continue to light our way but will require much of us along the road. We are not all going to get as much money as we think we need or deserve, but I would be very hopeful that we will have enough to live, to enjoy, and to be creative, even in a different kind of world.

The final question for this book is not whether you readers agree with me. (I would be highly flattered if someone would write a diametrically opposed book.) The final question is how all of you take the biblical material, relate it to your experience, understanding, and visions, and apply it to the world in which you live. How you learn to handle your money in terms of expectations and results is what really counts. If this book has provided you with some new data and some new thoughts about money, then my writing and your reading will have been pleasing in the sight of God, and for the benefit of the human race, which must learn to live with its money but not for it.